Beautiful Scars of Hope

By: Roxanne Holt

Foreword By: Clint Crawford

Dedicated in Loving Memory Of:

Ladell Peter Willis III

My oldest brother…. My HERO.

Foreword

Hope. Something the world needs more of, especially in these times we live in. Insight is something else we could benefit from, especially when it comes to addiction. In this book, Roxanne Holt offers these, in a very real, very honest, very courageous way. In this book the reader will find both as Roxanne talks about her story, from her early days growing up, to active addiction, to the trauma which happened during her active addiction, and to recovery.

As a therapist, who has worked in the addiction field for years, I have been vexed repeatedly by the overall treatment approach to treating females. It seems as though many, if not most therapists and treatment centers do not want to really get down to working on the hard things, the real things, that come up for females in active addiction and in early recovery. Another problem I have found is that often times neither do other people in recovery such as a lot of sponsors. Let's face it. It is uncomfortable. There is subject matter found in the lives of females struggling with addiction that is hard to talk about. Yet, if they do not have an avenue to talk about it, to face it, to process it, their chances at recovery are slim to none.

Roxanne faces these topics in a very real, and honest way. I have wanted a book like this to come out for years, to help me as a therapist, help the female patients I have worked with in the past, and will work with in the future. It offers hope, and it offers insight. If a person can grab ahold of those two things, they can recover. Roxanne Holt is a shining example of that.

Clint Crawford – April 2018

Preface

It was dark and a thick silence hung in the air….I sense him……I am paralyzed with fear. He's here. How is he here? I tell myself to be quiet, be still – I prayed as I held my breath for him to leave, to not hurt me again. I can feel his presence, I hear him breathing, I can smell his cheap cologne mixed with the smell of stale smoke and alcohol. Suddenly a sharp pain takes my breath from being hit on my back. I can tell I was struck with an object but cannot tell what; I just feel pain. Then just as quickly as that came, I was on my back. I feel his hands tightening around my throat. I can't breathe and the fear and anxiety of what was to come swell up inside of me. My body wanted to fight back, to run....but he was too strong, too powerful. I go limp and try to survive this attack hoping it ends as quickly as it came...I can barely speak however still try begging him...."NO" I scream, "PLEASE STOP, NO!"....then I sit straight up in my bed. I was breathing heavy, covered in sweat, relieved and confused at the same time. You're safe I told myself, you're safe, it was another nightmare. But where am I? It took a moment for my mind to clear and remember where I was. It was cold and dark and strangers were sleeping around me.....I was in detox.....again. My screaming woke an elderly woman sleeping in a bed against the far wall who glared at me with a look of pity and disgust. I looked down feeling full of shame and embarrassment. Briefly the thought of reliving my past trauma seemed better than my reality. Once I became aware of my surroundings the physical pain hit. I was in full withdrawal….everything hurt……I felt as if I needed to throw up but lacked the energy to move. I was willing to do anything in that moment to make it stop. I wanted to run, to escape, to find comfort in being numb from any thought or emotion, but I couldn't. Even if I could, where would I go? How would I get there? And what would I do – drinking and using stopped working long ago. Treatment? No, no, no! I know how to get sober, but I don't know how to STAY sober……why try?

There is a feeling that I have never been able to accurately describe with words that only others that have felt can truly understand. A darkness – a place of emptiness, fear with underlying apathy, helplessness, hopeless – a feeling of true desperation. When I speak to other alcoholics and addicts about this feeling there is an understanding in their eyes, free from judgement and a bond of compassion from knowing we both survived after going to that place of darkness.

That is where I was.

How did this become my life? How did I get here....why??? Now what???

    I *HAVE* to get sober, I *HAVE* to do this, my kids *NEED* me.....but I don't want to.....I don't think I can....what will happen if I fail? This was not my first trip to this particular detox facility or my first time going to treatment for that matter, but I was out of options, money and alone. I had hurt and alienated everyone who had ever loved or cared about me and was on my own this time…..so afraid…..HOPELESS.

Throughout my journey in recovery I have found HOPE. I have learned how to face my demons without drowning them in alcohol or numbing myself with drugs. I have learned and gained perspective about the journey my loved ones have been on as well. In the early days of recovery and treatment I was unable to see and believe in my future and would it be worth the work of surrendering and finally truly trying. I wanted to capture aspects of my journey for others in hopes that it inspires them to get honest and find hope in their own recovery. To speak bluntly and honestly about challenges women face in recovery and how I found to best navigate them. To tell you all the things they don't tell you about rehab and treatment but they should. To share my transformation of feeling broken, damaged and unworthy to seeing strength, power and beauty in myself. To inspire other alcoholics and addicts to at least believe that I believe until you are able to for yourself..... we CAN and DO recover!

Introduction

My name is Roxanne and I am an addict and an alcoholic. I don't claim to be an expert by any stretch of the imagination on recovery - however I have experience that I hope sharing will help other women relate to and allow them to take an honest look at their thinking and their own stories and find hope and maybe some helpful suggestions in their recovery. I have been sexually, mentally, emotionally and physically abused. Cheated on, widowed at the age of 31 with two young children, was in an extremely abusive relationship which ended with me in the hospital and him in prison. I've suffered concussions, broken bones, and shattered teeth. Been raped, beaten, held down and burned with cigarettes, sodomized and much, much more. Then entered a co-dependent relationship that's sole purpose was to support one another in using successfully. Throughout this whole period, I was also dealing with my oldest brother/best friend suffering with terminal brain cancer. My favorite thing to say at one point was "If you had been through what I've been through, you'd be drunk/high too". And I believed it. It was subconscious at first, but I found that being a victim and feeling valid in that self-righteous anger allowed me to live with my actions during active addiction. I have struggled with anxiety and depression, as well as PTSD, due to my trauma. Yes, I have experienced some horrible things in my life, but NONE of them are an excuse to drink or use. Today I am clean, sober, happy and healthy. God willing I will have four years sober in October of this year.....and never thought I could be where I am today. There is hope for every one of us -- we are ALL walking and talking miracles!

In writing this book, I aim to give an honest and open reference for women in recovery; the realities we face when getting clean and sober. I share my experiences along my journey simply as a reference point to relate to my thinking, actions, mistakes, insight, etc. There are topics that get touched on in early recovery, however people avoid discussing in detail. Let's just be honest....in getting sober we have to deal with life on life's terms and with that comes sober parenting, maintaining a program, relationships, intimacy vs.

sex, rebuilding trust, etc., etc. I was so grateful when someone was able to speak to me bluntly about things I needed to hear, so I am hoping this helps others in the same stages of their recovery.

When discussing this book with loved ones it was mentioned, "But Roxanne your children and family will all probably read this one day". My response to that is yes, but they also lived it. And a few details of how it was isn't the focus of this book. It is where I am now and how I got there and continue to "live recovery" every day

to maintain it. My reality is my reality and those who love me, see strength in my story rather than pain.....as my Daddy loves to say, "....But look where we are now".

My Story

Experience, Strength, and Hope

Throughout this book as I address various issues and challenges women face in recovery, I will also expand on aspects of my story, my insight, thinking, etc. However, when telling my story with others in recovery I was taught to share my experience, strength, and hope. What it was like, what happened, and what it is like now. Although I was also taught to stay in the solution, it is important to "qualify" yourself first by sharing some of your experience in active addiction. This allows other addicts and alcoholics the ability to relate to you, your thinking, and your actions. Once they can relate to you they judge themselves less and find strength and hope from how you have overcome things and are happy today by seeing that recovery is possible for them too. For someone not in recovery, maybe a family member or loved one of an addict or alcoholic, it provides a picture of what addiction is like and possibly provides some insight and understanding.

I usually start my story with my sobriety date of October 10, 2014. I am involved in a 12-step program, I have a sponsor, my sponsor has a sponsor, I am a member of a home group and hold a service position in that group. Although I am not directly identifying the 12-step program I am affiliated with out of respect to the traditions, I think it is important to say that, because my connection and involvement with my program is a large part of why I am still sober today.

I was born in Georgia in 1980; I am 37 years old. I grew up with two older brothers; they are 6 and 8 years older than me. My oldest brother Pete was (and still is) my hero. He had the biggest heart of anyone I've ever known and later in life a faith that inspired me to finally develop a personal relationship with God. My other brother Pat was "cool". He was usually in some sort of trouble; always got a lot of attention from girls; popular and everyone liked being around him. I looked up to both my brothers and there was an element of me that wanted to be like both of them. My parents met when they were young and have been together ever since; they have been married now 46 years. Although I believe that every family has some level of dysfunction, for all intent and purpose, I had a "normal" childhood.

My father was in the Army, and shortly after I was born we were transferred to Germany and lived there until I was 4 years old. From there we moved to Maryland where I spent the majority of my elementary school years, before moving home to Georgia where he retired. With me being the youngest I was not moved around nearly as much as my brothers. I moved back to Georgia the summer before 5th grade; I was 10 years old. Growing up with two older brothers and a military father I was not equipped with many coping skills. My father's thinking was if you want something, you work hard and make it happen. He believed in will power and having pride in what you do. The only "coping skills" he provided me really at a young age was to, "Put your big girl britches on, and deal with it". My mother is old school southern and it was always important to her to present well. I was her only daughter and she instilled in me the importance to "be pleasing" and we joked later in my life about a song that referenced, "Hide your crazy and act like a lady". An old saying that comes to mind is to, "Not air your dirty laundry". My mother was an only child and lost her mother in a car accident as a teenager; her father, my grandfather, was an alcoholic. I was her baby and only girl, so my mother spoiled me a lot growing up and lived vicariously through me throughout my youth. Although we would clash, argue and butt heads regularly, there was never a doubt that my mother would do absolutely anything I needed. I knew I was loved by both parents growing up. Regardless of what was going on however, it was known that I was to be well behaved and not embarrass my parents, it wouldn't be tolerated.

I started playing sports when I was very young because my older brothers did, and because both of my parents worked, and my brothers were "stuck" watching me. I became their tag along of sorts, so I started playing sports too. I started out with competitive swimming, I was racing at the age of 5. My oldest brother Pete was a lifeguard and took me to work with him in the afternoons, so I became the neighborhood "pool rat". As I got older he became one of my swim team coaches and my swimming, and success in the sport became a big part of our relationship. I later started playing tennis, basketball, and was a cheerleader, all while continuing to swim throughout my childhood. My senior superlative in high school was, "Most Athletic" and that was my identity while growing up. I was good at sports. It came naturally to me and I was diligent at practicing and working hard to remain competitive and continuously show improvement. I did well in school and my parents were proud of the young woman I was becoming. Because I was so involved with sports I had several practices after school and I think that is what kept me from going too far with my drinking and using at a young age, because ultimately, I knew, if I messed up too bad, I wouldn't be able to play. I was a star student athlete, an honor graduate, the pageant winner and "queen" of my high school during the week and partied with my friends on the weekends.

    The town in Georgia I grew up in was very small; we only had one red light back then. There wasn't much to do so teenagers usually went "cruising" or tail gated in farmers fields or hung out at each other's houses socializing. With that socializing there was always drinking. I started drinking in middle school and then experimenting with marijuana. I honestly didn't think there was anything really wrong with what I was doing; I knew my parents didn't want me to, but I was doing what all the other kids were doing, what I had seen my brother Pat do with his friends and thought it was "normal". I did notice at some point that I enjoyed it a little more than some of my friends, but at the time I just thought that meant I was "cooler" than they were and started hanging out with the people that did like it as much as me. This continued throughout high school and I later left home and went to college at The University of Georgia (Go Dawgs!). I didn't go to UGA for any academic reasons or programs they offered. I was actually an undecided major my entire freshman year. To this day if you ask my mother what my major was, she will tell you I majored in keg stands and packing coolers. I went to The University of Georgia because it was about 2 hours from home and my strict retired military father. I had good friends that were going to school there too and at the time UGA was ranked in the top 10 party schools in the nation, so naturally I thought I'd fit in. I had been offered sports scholarships at some smaller schools in Georgia, however decided to stop playing sports in college because all of the practices were interfering with my social life. I remember freshman year buying a t-shirt that read, "University of Georgia….producing the best educated alcoholics since 1785". In retrospect it is funny, if I had only known then what I know now, but of course I thought, "See…. these are my people".

I was very aware of alcoholism. I had grandfathers on both sides, great uncles and my great grandfather that were all alcoholics (it was quickly pointed out to me however, that I was the first female in our family to ever have, "This problem"). Although my family was full of alcoholics and I had always heard it, "Could be hereditary", I again thought I was doing what I was supposed to be doing in college; everyone drinks and parties in college. It eventually got to a point where I was missing classes, my grades were suffering, and I was drinking in the mornings sometimes rather than just when I was going out at night. I remember my sophomore year having someone push an AA (Alcoholics Anonymous) number under my bedroom door and I just thought at the time someone was trying to be funny. All I knew of Alcoholics Anonymous I had heard from other people or saw in shows or movies and honestly thought of it as a bunch of old men sitting around smoking. I started having trouble in relationships, roommate and boyfriend drama, and started feeling depressed. It was towards the end of my sophomore year that I came home to visit one weekend and just told my parents I didn't want to go back. I had called my advisor and found out I could "take a break" for a year without having to reapply. My parents were shocked and disappointed but wanted to help me. They of course did not know that my drinking had escalated to the point it had and was driving most of my problems and behavior. They agreed however and told me if I was taking a break from classes they were not going to continue to pay for me to have an apartment in Athens, that I would have to move back home and get a job. I agreed and back home I went, thinking I would later return, but never did.

When I came home and started working I met the man that later became my husband. When we first met I remember he had a cooler full of beer in the back of his truck and I asked if he was headed to a cookout or something and he said, "No, I keep cold beer back there just in case". As crazy as that sounds, at 19 I thought, "Cool, we could probably hang out". That initial relationship grew quickly into a friendship and romance that was somewhat of a whirlwind. After 4 months of dating he proposed and shortly after a year from meeting him we were married; I had just turned

21. We tried to have children right away because he was 5 years older than me and wanted to have our children young, so we could be active with them growing up. So, I had my first son at 22 years old and then my second son at 25 years old. This was the period of my life where I convinced myself I was not an alcoholic and I was able to "control" my drinking. I didn't drink at all really for years, just here and there when I had a break from parenting or a weekend away. Now mind you, on those weekends I was blackout drunk, but felt valid in doing it and that I "deserved" to have a good time. After all, I was "that mom". I attended every school function, usually with cupcakes in hand, I was "team mom" for not one but two baseball teams my children played on while my husband

was the coach. I volunteered with helping kids read at the elementary school, chaperoned every field trip, all the while working a full-time job that I had promoted up in and become very successful in spite of not completing my degree. Why not have "fun" when I get a weekend off? Only my version of what constituted fun was much different than your average person. My husband still drank throughout those years, but not to a point that I ever felt it was in excess; it was normal to drink to me. Once my boys got a little older and a little more self-sufficient I can remember having a drink here and there in the evenings with my husband once the boys had gone to bed and that slowly became more, and more often.

Now you'll notice up to this point of my story I didn't reference any type of relationship with God. Because we moved around when I was younger, we never regularly attended church. I remember when we would come home to Georgia to visit we may go to church with my great aunt and we prayed when it was time to eat, but that was about it. I believed there was a God, I just didn't know much of anything about Him. I always claimed to be a logical thinker like my father and could believe in whatever I wanted to believe in without going into a church. Honestly, I thought all of "those people" were fake and hypocritical. I thought of God a bit like Santa Claus, he probably had a good list and a bad list, and I was on the bad list and not willing to change my behavior consistently to be on the "good list". But at 27 years old I found out my oldest brother Pete was diagnosed with brain cancer and it rocked my world. I can remember crying and sitting on my back porch telling God if He were real I didn't want any part of Him or His plan; I didn't understand it and it wasn't fair. "Not Pete", I remember thinking, "He was so good and pure, he had 5 children, a wife and his entire life ahead of him". I wished it could be me, "I deserved it, he didn't", I told myself. So, I made a conscious decision at that point to not communicate with, or "buy into" the concept of God; I was too angry, hurt and scared.

My brother was given 2-6 months to live without extensive surgery. He consented to the surgery but suffered a debilitating stroke during the procedure. He had to accept medical retirement from a job he loved and moved back home to Georgia, so our family could help take care of him. Everything he knew was changed in an instant, but his faith never wavered. He ended up living 9 long years after that and passed away December of 2016. He actually published a book about his unyielding faith while living with terminal cancer; his testimony helped so many people. I feel blessed that I was able to spend his last years with him sober and regain our relationship I gave up while in active addiction. But of course, when I was 27 I didn't know the future and was just angry at God and scared of losing my big brother.

Throughout my marriage we had ups and downs and normal growing pains, but about ten and a half years into my marriage I found out my husband had cheated on me. I was heartbroken. At this point, because of our relationship issues, if I was working late and knew the boys would already be in bed by the time I arrived home I would stop at a bar on the way home from work with friends to avoid facing my husband and our marital problems. I was so angry, but like any alcoholic I am an insecure egomaniac! It was more that my pride was hurt than my marriage vows being broken. I can remember thinking….."You cheated on me? Do you have any idea how many times I could have cheated on you and didn't?" Sounds crazy I know, but that's what I was thinking at the time. He was not wanting to divorce, but to try and save our marriage. He became willing to do things he wouldn't participate in when we had discussed it in the past, like marriage counseling, etc.

It was right around Thanksgiving when all of this came about, so we agreed he would stay in our home through Christmas for the kids then he would get an apartment to provide me with some much needed space and we would go from there. And that's what we did. The week following Christmas he signed a 6-month lease on an apartment and moved out of our home. I had met various men and friends socially when going out in the evenings and would talk to them about my marital woes and look to them for comfort. However, I never entertained any of those relationships as being something serious. I was still so angry and hurt about his infidelity I felt valid in flirting with other men when we were separated. A few weeks after moving out, my husband was supposed to pick the kids up from daycare and school and I could not get in touch with him. After several calls and frustration, we learned my husband had passed away in his apartment. It wasn't due to anything drug or alcohol related, he had a heart attack in his sleep and passed of natural causes at the age of 36. He was a big guy and had a family history of heart disease on both sides of his family, but none of us ever expected something like that to happen. So, there I was, 31 years old and a widow with two boys who had just turned 6 and 9 years old.

I didn't know what to do, how to feel, how to cope, I was completely overwhelmed. I was hurt, still angry, felt guilty for being angry still, felt guilty he was alone in that apartment when he died since I was the one that asked him to move out. What if he had been home or with me? Maybe I could have done something to help him? What do I do about his apartment? How will I pay our bills? And my poor boys…..what will I tell them? How can they understand? What will this do to them at such a young age? Regardless of any of our problems, my boys adored him, and he was always a good father. I cannot put into words the emotional roller coaster I went on the months following his passing. His mistress was in attendance at his funeral (of course she wasn't aware I knew who she was; I only found out when the coroner provided his cell phone to me). His mother and father were heartbroken, and his mother blamed me from the stress of the separation. My boys didn't know why Daddy left home, they just knew I had asked him to leave and they blamed me too. I was in a place where I would just sit and cry and wonder, "What in the world will I do now?"

Early on I continued working for a few months and my mother took early retirement to help me with my children. I couldn't sleep much at all and when I did, I slept on the couch, I couldn't bring myself to sleep in our bed at that point. I can vividly remember one night lying on the couch and could see a bottle of rum on top of the refrigerator and thinking, "I could just take a couple of shots and I might be able to sleep a little". And it spiraled from there. It didn't take long before I was drinking more and more to be able to sleep and it started to affect my work performance. I was late, hungover when arriving to work, not focused throughout the day, etc., etc. Rather than admit these problems were due to my drinking I blamed them on my emotional state and the loss of my husband. I didn't equate my problems with my drinking at that point. I quit working shortly thereafter stating that, "my boys need me right now", and financially I was able to due to life insurance monies and survivor benefits. Once I stopped working my drinking escalated even faster.

During the period of time my husband and I were separated, one of the men I met at the bar was still talking to me pretty regularly. After the funeral and things settled down some, he was there, all the time. He presented as being supportive and compassionate, however I later learned he knew I had inherited a life insurance policy and just needed someone to help fund his crack habit that I was unaware of when we met. He was an escape for me. He liked to drink and have fun, he told me I was beautiful and made me feel good in a time when I was not able to do that for myself. He was the complete opposite of my husband. He was 4 years younger than me, tattoos from head to toe and from up north originally. My family thought I had lost my mind altogether. First, because I was already "dating" and hanging around another man so soon after my husband passed away, and also because he was nothing like anyone I had ever shown interest in before. They would try to talk sense into me and confront me on my behavior, but I was not willing to listen. I didn't want to hear someone telling me they didn't like what I was doing or that I needed to change and face reality, so I just ran from the situation. The new boyfriend and I moved away to New York, and of course, took my boys with us to "start over". At this point he had re-introduced me to some of the drugs I dabbled with while I was in college as well as introducing me to crack cocaine. And I loved it; I felt wonderful the first time I used it and I learned cocaine helped me to be able to drink more, which was usually my goal.

Once away from all of my family and the few "friends" I still had back home, things got much worse, much quicker. He had been physically abusive once or twice prior to moving to New York but blamed it on the drug use and promised he would stop once we moved. That of course did not happen. Although during my marriage I had experienced some mental and emotional abuse, my husband had never physically hit me before. Honestly, growing up with two brothers and being a tall athletic woman, I falsely believed I would never be, "that girl". But before I knew it, I was. The abuse escalated quickly, and my drinking increased right along with it to cope with my situation and reality. Throughout those months I had a broken arm, shattered teeth, concussions, countless bruises, had been beaten, thrown, held down and burned with cigarettes, raped, sodomized, and my spirit broken. My self-esteem was nonexistent, and I just stayed drunk most of the time. The day I finally tried to leave was very violent and I don't go into a lot of detail usually when telling my story other than to say that it ended with me in a hospital and him in prison. He is still there today and will hopefully be there for many years due to the things that happened that day.

Once I was in the hospital I called my parents and they drove all throughout the night from Georgia to come and "rescue" me. They were destroyed emotionally once they learned everything that had happened and did not know what to do. They were aware I was drinking but had no idea how heavily. I had progressed to the point of being physically dependent. I would wake with shakes and have withdrawal symptoms when I attempted not to drink for any period of time. They came and helped me get things in order and brought me back to Georgia. I believed once I was safely back home and away from my abuser I would be able to stop drinking; that I wouldn't need to drink to cope anymore, but I was wrong. Although I was away from my abuser, my thinking and coping skills had not changed. I still relived my trauma during night terrors and still had not dealt with my unresolved feelings and grieved the loss of my husband. I was "successful" for a short period of time at hiding my drinking, but that did not last long. Once it became apparent to those around me that I was drinking, I realized if I brought up being a widow or a victim of domestic violence people became uncomfortable enough or felt sorry for me enough that they would back off and I could continue to drink without anyone holding me accountable. My tagline became, "If you had been through what I had been through, you would be drunk too". Sadly, once I saw how effective it was, I used it to "protect" my addiction and continue in active addiction without people making me feel bad about what I was doing and just leave me alone.

After a few months of being home in Georgia I progressed in my drinking to where I was drinking about a half-gallon of rum a day. One day my sons came in my room to find me passed out on my bed and could not wake me up. They were terrified, especially given the way their father passed away. They didn't know what to do, so they called their Granddaddy to ask for help. My Dad came over and collected me and took me to the hospital and I landed in my first detox center. They talked to me at detox about going to treatment, but I was completely against it. I believed that I had gotten out of control and become physically dependent on alcohol, however didn't think it was a problem in the past and I had managed it successfully. I believed at the time, that because of everything I had been through, I just took things too far and once it was out of my system I would be fine. This is nothing but denial and delusion, but at the time I believed it. I talked my poor father (who was always my biggest enabler) into not going to treatment, rather that we could just go to the beach for a week or so with my Mom and the children and I could regain my serenity and would be fine. And that's what we did. My father meant well, he is a fixer, he felt guilty for all that I had experienced and not being able to "protect" me and the boys from it all and wanted to help me get back on track; he just didn't know what to do and wanted to believe me. So off to the beach we went. Including the days I was in detox and then at the beach with my family I was only sober a total of

15 days, I was drunk the day after we returned from the beach.

It took about another 2 months of being drunk, hurting the people I loved the most, an involuntary commitment that my parents had a judge sign off on when I was in DT's (delirium tremens) and having my parents physically remove my children from our home (although they had not legally attempted to have them removed from my custody at that point). I landed in detox again. During those couple of months prior to making it to detox, I was also introduced to heroin for the first time. A "friend" of a "friend" came by my house stating he was concerned about me. He heard from my friend that I was drinking a lot, getting sloppy and not able to take care of my kids. He also heard I was seeking out cocaine again to help me manage my drinking more successfully like I thought I had in the past. He told me he had, "Something that would make me feel the way I wanted to without being sloppy drunk and smelling like liquor", so I thought ok I'll try it, "what is it?" I asked. He then pulled out a "rig" (a syringe or needle) and told me heroin. I was terrified initially and thought, "no way!". I thought of heroin as a "scary" and "serious" drug and had this horrible image of who and what a heroin addict was, and told him, "I don't do needles". My thinking was that sure I had done some drugs, but drinking was the only thing I believed I had a problem with, and needed, without being able to stop. But, I was drunk of course having this conversation, so it wasn't long before he convinced me, and I stuck my arm out. So, the very first time I ever tried heroin, it was with a needle and I loved it. I remember where I was standing, what I was wearing and the feeling I had throughout my entire body. Nothing hurt, I wasn't consumed with my thoughts and misery, I was numb and felt free….which is ironic since I later became a prisoner to heroin and it then consumed all of my thoughts. Thankfully, at that point I did not have the access or enough money to start using heroin daily or in large amounts, so I continued to drink and use cocaine primarily. After my children were gone from the home for a little over a week, I became very depressed one day while I was drinking and called my father saying I needed help.

He was very angry and frustrated with me and said, "If I wanted help I needed to go get it". I managed to drive myself to the hospital and passed out in the parking deck after finishing the pint of rum I bought for the ride there. Once I woke up later that day and finally made it to the hospital my Dad came and helped me get back into detox and offered to pay for me to go to my first treatment center. I no longer had any type of health insurance, so they were going to have to pay out of pocket for me to go.

At this point I was unhappy and knew I needed to do something different, but I couldn't imagine a future with no drugs or alcohol. My parents told me not going to treatment was not an option this time and threatened to take steps to remove my children from my care legally if I did not agree to go to some sort of treatment. So, I agreed reluctantly, but had demands prior to being "willing" to go. I say willing, but of course the mere fact that I had demands means I wasn't fully willing. I would go to treatment IF it was somewhere local, I had access to a phone and computer, I was able to see my kids regularly, I could smoke as much as I wanted to, etc., etc. My poor parents were so scared and were just so grateful that I was finally going to treatment they complied with my demands, again doing the best thing they knew to help me at the time. They called and arranged everything for me, paid for my treatment and off I went to a six-week program in my hometown.

Again, I wasn't at a point where I really wanted to be sober yet, but I wanted my parents to not be mad with me anymore, my kids to be back with me, and knew my way wasn't really working. I somehow thought going to treatment would teach me how to manage my drinking "successfully" again. I didn't want to let go of my only coping skill, but I got to a point where I wanted my consequences to go away. While in this treatment I was introduced to 12 step meetings for the first time. I was a little intimidated initially and entered meetings comparing myself to others rather than identifying, in an effort to prove to myself I was not like them, I wasn't an alcoholic, I had just let things get out of control for a while and could use this treatment to fix that. I remember calling my Dad at one point and telling him I didn't really belong there because I was around heroin addicts and I was, "just an alcoholic". Of course, I had used heroin and tried just about every other drug out there by that point but didn't think I had a problem with those; that was just recreational in my mind. The only thing that caused me to have major consequences, extreme physical detox, and I NEEDED daily, was alcohol, so that was my problem. I somehow thought that made me better than some of my peers in treatment and meetings because alcohol was legal and more socially acceptable. All of this is again insane thinking and rationalization. If I admitted I was like them and that I was an alcoholic and drug addict, that meant I had to do something about it and would never be able to use again, and I was not ready to do that at that point.

So, of course I did what I have always done in the past. You take away all of my "coping skills" (drugs and alcohol) and I have to feel feelings I have been running from and going numb to for so long and I go to the next best thing, my other "drug of choice" so to speak, men. When I was about two weeks sober, I met a man in a meeting. He was about 7 months sober and had just completed a six-month treatment and in my mind that was a really long time and couldn't imagine being sober that long myself. I was full of guilt and shame at the time and couldn't even look myself in the eye when looking in the mirror in the mornings. I learned the difference of guilt and shame. Guilt is feeling bad about something specific I did to someone, "Look what I did to them". But shame is getting to the point where you feel bad about who you are, "Look what I have become". I was so full of both. When I met this guy in a meeting he validated me and told me the things I couldn't believe or do for myself at that time. He told me I was beautiful when I couldn't see anything beautiful in myself, he told me he loved me when I couldn't love myself, he made me feel good physically when I didn't have drugs and alcohol to make me feel good anymore, he was big and strong and made me feel safe and secure when I was still struggling with PTSD and trauma from my time in New York. He was a distraction for me and an easy way to validate myself through someone else instead of learning how to do that for myself. Of course, I didn't realize all of those things at that time, I just thought it was love. I thought we would be "that couple" in the program. I envisioned a happy ending with program cookouts in the backyard and being happy. I even rationalized that because I was an alcoholic and he was a heroin addict it would be fine, "Because we won't even tempt each other". Oh, how wrong I was. Everyone around me was telling me it wasn't a good idea and I shouldn't do it, but I thought I knew best and wouldn't listen to the people trying to help me.

A couple of weeks after I completed my six-week treatment program, he moved in with me. Although my parents were concerned, they knew little about recovery and believed me when I told them it was a positive thing and since we were both in the program we would be able to keep each other sober. They were so scared of me relapsing and grateful that I was sober, they just wanted to believe me and didn't know what else to do. I was in my own home and paying my own bills, so they thought there wasn't much they could do to object. I honestly cannot tell you exactly how long I stayed sober; including the time I was in treatment it was somewhere between 4 and 5 months. It was around the time I had to go and testify in New York for the trial and face my abuser. Although I was "dry" and had not drank or drugged for several months, I had not changed anything about myself; work any steps, learn new coping skills, anything. So, in the face of dealing with feelings and emotions I was not equipped to face and handle, "life on life's terms," I turned back to the what I knew; going numb.

Although out of respect for traditions I am not affiliating myself with a particular 12-step program, anyone that has been in or around recovery has heard about the "13th step". I had to select a sponsor because it was a requirement of treatment, so I selected someone I was able to manipulate and wouldn't challenge me. I halfway worked the first step but couldn't accept at that point that I was powerless; simply that I had allowed things to become unmanageable. When looking at the remaining steps I saw God in multiple places and had already decided that I didn't have a desire to know the God I thought they were talking about. I also saw self-reflection, acceptance and accountability in the remaining steps, all of which I was not willing to face at that time, so I simply sat in meetings and let the newest man in my life become my program. That was a familiar and easy distraction when I was not willing to change. I still thought, "I got this, I can manage myself, there is nothing I've ever really wanted to do in the past that I had not been able to be successful at".

When facing my past and testifying in front of my abuser during the trial, I was on the stand for 4 days and had to relive a very dark and painful time of my life and was not equipped with tools and coping skills to maintain my sobriety due to my lack of effort in working a program. I sat and listened to hours of phone calls between my abuser and his family and friends where I was completely unaware that I was being followed leading up to the trial. I had to hear detailed plans to lure me to certain areas and how they planned to kill me and bury my body where no one would ever find it. The phrase I would hear him say over and over after was, "no face, no case, get rid of the bitch". Although following that trial he was found guilty on all charges, I then lived in fear and was paranoid about being followed or targeted. I can remember someone in recovery telling me very early on that if I wanted to stay sober I would have to forgive my abuser and at that time forgiveness still equated me saying what he had done to me was ok, so I didn't think I would ever be able to forgive him and therefore never be able to maintain sobriety. I used that as an excuse as to why it wasn't possible for me to be successful in achieving recovery. I stopped believing in my ability to be happy and have a sense of "normalcy"; I gave up.

When I relapsed, I did it with the man I was living with. I realize now that all of the people I associated with and the "friends" I kept around me were always just a little "sicker" than I thought I was. That helped me to live with and be ok with my own actions and still have a feeling of helping and trying to save other people rather than looking at my own problems. I don't blame him for my relapse. I knew what I was doing and made the choice to do it. He was an addict and sick too; we just became very codependent, unhealthy and helped each other use. We relapsed on heroin and I remember having a conversation with him where we said that, "as long as we didn't use needles we would be ok and be able to manage it without it getting out of control". I was working again and had a good job and didn't want to mess that up. I jokingly said that we would just be "weekend warriors". Well, that only lasted one weekend and then we were using heroin IV daily.

That continued for about another year and a half. I had been to the doctor at one point and my parents were aware I had a large stomach ulcer due to my heavy drinking in the past. So, I started to isolate and attempt to hide my using. As I started to lose significant weight and look unhealthy I blamed my stomach ulcer and not being able to keep food down, etc. I later learned that my mother kept telling my father she thought something was wrong, and that I was using, and my father would defend me telling her, "She wouldn't lie to me". And although they were familiar with the signs of me drinking, they weren't familiar with heroin use or the signs to look for.

One day I was completely out of options. None of the 5 dealers I frequented had anything, I was out of cigarettes, my battery was dead in my truck and it was out of gas (not to mention I had no car insurance, an expired tag and it was currently on a repo list). I had no money, my bank account was over $1,000 in the red. There was nothing left in the kitchen other than the roaches that were covering anything that would stand still, and still I was trying to figure out a way to get some dope and stop feeling sick. The man I was living and using with was dope sick too. Frustrated and before I could manage a plan for the day, he broke down and called his mother and admitted everything. I knew it wouldn't be long before my parents were contacted and filled in, so I thought it best for me to "wave the white flag", tell them myself what I had been doing and the position I found myself in and ask for help. I called my mother and she came over and picked me up (I no longer let my parents inside my house due to having sold almost everything in it; it was filthy, and the kitchen had been overrun with roaches).

My kids, sadly, were still with me and living in the home too. She drove me to her home and I sat on the back porch and told her I was addicted to heroin, sick and wanted help. Still at this point not believing I was really done with drinking and using, just out of options and maybe if she got me to the hospital they could at least give me something to help with the pain I was in. She was disgusted and irate with me. My father was a few hours away golfing with my great uncle, so she called him and interrupted his trip telling him he needed to come home immediately and what was happening. The man I was with was not wanting treatment. He had been multiple times in the past and said, "I know what to do already, I just need to detox". On the way to the hospital he asked my mother to drop him off at his Aunt's house, who was also in recovery and she would help him detox. I could almost see steam coming out of my mother's ears she was so angry. She did drop him off, glad and hoping she would never lay eyes on him again. I can remember him crying and telling me he was scared for me to go to treatment because he was afraid after I got sober I wouldn't want him anymore. We separated there with intentions of both getting well and then continuing our relationship.

I don't remember everything about the ride to the hospital, except that my mother was livid with me, for good reason. I remember her saying that, "I knew something was going on and I have been praying that it would come to light". And my thinking was so twisted at the time I remember thinking, "Well, I came clean about what I was doing and asked for help, you should be happy then". And that made sense to me at the time. My thinking had become so self-absorbed and selfish I really couldn't understand why people still cared anymore; I wasn't hurting anyone but myself……again, insane thinking. What stands out the most was how upset she was about what I had been doing, her trying to wrap her mind around the fact that I was addicted to heroin. She told me, "It was bad enough to have people find out you were an alcoholic the first time you went to treatment, but now this?!?! HEROIN???". Which I understood. Even though I had become a heroin addict, I had this image of what and who an IV heroin addict was and it wasn't me…..but that is what is so cunning and baffling about this disease. It doesn't discriminate, and honestly, I believe that the fact that I didn't fit the stereotypical image of an addict initially helped me hide my disease even longer. But at this point there was no denying what I had become.

Once I arrived at the hospital my Mom stayed only until my father arrived. She told me she, "Wasn't going through this again" and remembered how ugly I had gotten in the past once I started detoxing. She was going to go pick my boys up from school and my father could, "Deal with me". When my father arrived, I can clearly remember the look on his face. It wasn't like it had been in the past. He looked disappointed and afraid for me more than he had in the past, but I don't know how to explain it other than he looked tired and broken. I remember him saying, "Roxanne, it's time…..you are 34 years old, you're too old for this shit and have children that need you". He looked at me and told me, "I love you and I hope you get better, but I can't do this anymore. I will take care of your boys because they deserve better, but I'm done helping you. If you want treatment, you figure it out". And once he knew I was in the process of being transported to the state-run detox center, again, he left. I couldn't believe it……."I'm Roxanne". Dad had never turned his back on me, or told me no. I was hurt, angry, and deep down didn't really believe him. I was detoxing hard by then and was in so much pain I didn't focus on what he said or really believe it, I just wanted relief. I thought he was really mad, would go home and cool off and then come see me in detox and we would come up with a plan to fix everything....again. Only that didn't happen. I would call, and he would continue to tell me the same thing. So, while in detox I grabbed the resource book they had and called a place I learned of while I was in treatment the first time and had met a few people that had gone to treatment there. I explained my situation to the girl on the other end of the line. I told her I was negative in my bank account; however, I still receive survivor benefits from my husband passing away and the money would hit my account in about a week and asked if I could go ahead and come and pay them then. Their fee was $800 a month, which covered food and everything. She placed me on a quick hold before returning and telling me that I would be able to come.

I was relieved at first for having an option of somewhere to go, but fully believed that since I had shown some sort of an effort and initiative that my father would believe that I really wanted help this time and would now be willing to come to my rescue as he had always done in the past. I called to tell him what I had accomplished expecting his tone to change, but it didn't, he simply said, "Good, I will be willing to give you a ride from detox to there to drop you off, but that is all". I couldn't believe how angry he was this time. I believed my mother must have turned him against me because he had never been this way towards me before; I was his baby. But I later learned my mother had nothing to do with it, other than to support his decision and be willing to take care of my children because I was unable to. It was unfair for me to direct so much of my anger towards her in retrospect. After a couple more days in detox I was ready to leave. It was cold, crowded, the food was horrible, and I couldn't smoke. I thought since I was going to a long-term treatment (minimum of six months) that my parents would be ok with me leaving detox a day early; they had always let me when I asked in the past. I called my dad and when he said no, he would pick me up the next day when I was scheduled to be released, I got angry (as if I had any right to be angry with them about anything). I remember yelling at him and saying, "This is crazy, I shouldn't have to be here another entire day for some vitamin I don't even need for alcohol detox Dad! I'm not even really an alcoholic anymore, I'm a heroin addict!!!". He paused, then simply said, "Roxanne I was just at your house and there were 15 empty liquor bottles stuffed down in your couch". I responded by simply saying, "Yeah, but they are pints; hell Daddy, I use to drink a handle (half-gallon) a day, that's not a drinking problem that's just waiting on a re-up!". He hung up on me at that point. The crazy thing to me is that I thought that was a valid argument at that time, in comparison to the amount I drank in the past, I didn't see a problem and had decided that heroin was my only issue now.....denial, again.

The following day my father arrived to transport me to treatment with one small Nike duffel bag my mother had packed with a few outfits and changes of underwear…..for a SIX MONTH treatment. He said, "You'll be fine, you need to be grateful she packed you anything and is taking care of your boys. If you need anything else, we'll send it later". And off we went. Before heading south my father did stop by his house and allow me to say goodbye to my boys, mostly because I believe he was afraid I would try to run if he didn't. I can remember them trying to be supportive of me, tell me they loved me and reassure me that they were "ok". No child should EVER feel obligated to do this for their mother, whose sole purpose is to protect THEM. But bless their hearts that is what they did. I can remember my youngest son Logan, he was only 8 at the time, telling me that, "Granny had already told him I was going to miss the holidays, but that it was ok because he would get to come visit me and celebrate with me where I was going". He didn't even really know where I was going, but he remembered me being in rehab before and just knew this time I would be there longer. He smiled and told me he hoped, "I felt better and that I liked it there." Then suddenly I saw this look of sadness come across his face as he teared up and realized, "You're not going to be here for my birthday, are you?" At that moment, six days sober, I felt emotions I had run from for a long time; pain, guilt, sadness, shame and so many more. I teared up, then attempted to put on a "brave face" for him and hugged him tight telling him that I would make sure we celebrated when he came to visit, but I could feel my heart breaking inside as I said it. I had failed him, both of them. Then I went upstairs to say goodbye to my brother Pete, my person, who had been fighting to live for years, as I wasted my life and health. I had not been to see him or visit him in a long time because I was too ashamed to look at him. I remember him crying and telling me, "Roxanne, I don't understand what you have been doing or why. I don't know what you are going to do while you are down there…..but PLEASE, just bring my sister back". In that moment with Pete and Logan, what they said to me motivated me more than any threat or consequences I have ever faced. I didn't want to hurt them or let them down anymore, I hated what I had become.

Me, in active addiction. July 2014, about two and a half months prior to going to treatment.

Me in sobriety. Present in my children's lives, a mother and GENUINELY happy

Chapter 1

Going to Treatment

Willingness doesn't mean you have to be enthusiastic....just be willing!

The drive is about two to two and a half hours from my hometown, but that day it took almost four hours before we arrived. My dad took this time and opportunity to talk to me. He was sounding more like the dad I knew then and I thought he had forgiven me. The truth is he hadn't, but he loved me and was so afraid I would back out and was terrified for me to not go to treatment. We had our first conversation about God that day.....ever. My father had been saved as a child, but at the age of 61 he re-dedicated himself to the Lord (I was in active addiction). I vaguely remember attending his baptism and had shot up before entering the church and nodded out on the pew. He and I had always "thought alike" in the past about all of the God business, but now he had changed. I didn't trust it or understand it really at the time, but I could tell he believed what he was saying, and I honestly became curious. Where I went to treatment was in a little town in South Georgia that I had never heard of before, purposely placed in the middle of nowhere. Along the way a bald eagle flew down and swooped in front of the truck; we were stunned. I had never seen one out in nature before, and my father told me he believed it was an omen. I remember him telling me, "Roxanne, I know you. You can come down here and make everyone love you and be running the place within a couple of weeks, OR this time you can try to get something from it and get better". And he was right, that is what I had always done before. I can get along in any situation when I need or want to and be successful, but I was never fully honest or allowed myself to become vulnerable. I would share some "big" things but held onto the things I was most afraid to face and was able to fake my way through treatment. But this time I thought, "Well….I am going to be stuck here for six months either way. I guess this time I can try to give it an honest effort. It probably won't work, but hell what do I have to lose".

I remember pulling up and several women sitting out on the front porch of the building in rocking chairs staring at me and trying to figure me out. I thought, "Ugh….women are such drama…..I get along better with men, this is going to be a long six months". The funny thing is I had always said that. I am into sports, a tom-boy, grew up with brothers and some of my best friends growing up were guys…..I thought I just got along with men better. But the reality is I looked to men for relationships because it was easier, and I felt validated. I had never learned how to really get along with other women…….the reality was simply that they were more challenging to manipulate. After we got in the office, my dad was very short. He asked the woman in the office if he needed to sign anything. I had already given him all of the passwords and access to my accounts to pay for my monthly fees and my house payment at home since he was no longer willing to assist me financially. After they said no, he dropped my bag with a loud bang on the floor of the office from his tall 6'6" frame, gave me a slap on the shoulder and said I'll see you later and walked out. I just looked to the floor, and stunned, the office manager asked me, "What in the world did you do to make him so angry??" I couldn't even answer her I was so ashamed of myself in that moment.

    I will go into more detail about my experiences and the changes in my thinking while I was in treatment in later chapters. But as much as I despised being there initially, I now think of that place as a second home and am so grateful that it helped me save my life. When I arrived at treatment I weighed 110 lbs. (I am 6'2" and didn't even think my bones weighed that little), my skin was gray from my organs beginning to fail, I had two black eyes from lack of sleep and malnutrition, I had a stomach ulcer covering over half of my stomach, my hair was falling out…..but most of all my eyes were empty…….. I was hopeless. I was actively dying, but still believed, "I got this". At that point my denial had become full delusion. In the face of overwhelming evidence that I didn't "have" anything, I still convinced myself that I did, that I was "ok". I called it heroin chic and thought anyone who said anything was just jealous because I was skinnier than they were……SICK thinking I know, but that's what I was telling myself. I remember every time in the past when someone had come and "collected" me and got me to a hospital, the nurses would always ask me if I was suicidal. I was usually angry at that point and am naturally a smart ass, so my response was usually, "No, why are you?". And although I was too chicken to commit suicide in the conventional way, I was doing it slowly with drugs. I can remember thinking at one point, "If I just overdose and they find me, everyone will think it was an accident", and then would be so angry when I woke up again the next day.

    I have a relationship with God today that I cherish and do not believe I would still be sober today without it. It was a slow process for me, however I believe that God places people in your life for a reason. When I arrived at treatment, I met someone I believe God placed there for me. She didn't belong in a long-term treatment center. She was a sweet older lady that had gotten a DUI over a year ago and placed on probation. She violated her probation by going outside of her boundary getting lunch on her way to an appointment without notifying her probation officer and ended up being mandated to a treatment center for six months with an ankle monitor. Again, she should not have been there; the poor woman had not even drunk any alcohol for over a year. But she was SO HAPPY; I mean annoyingly happy. I remember thinking when I first saw her, "No one is that happy in rehab……I bet she has a stash of something in the woods", so I decided to be friendly with her, just in case I happened to be right. And although I was right about her having something, I was wrong about what. It wasn't a stash of any drugs or alcohol, it was her faith.

I had always heard in my brief experience in the program that when choosing a sponsor, you should, "Look for someone who has what you want". That is kind of how I thought about her. She had a type of faith that I have never witnessed, and I watched her for a while to see if I believed it was real. And against everything I have ever told myself in the past, I DID believe it was real. And I wanted it. I didn't believe at that point it would ever feel "real" but I was curious enough to be interested in learning more and giving it a shot. I wanted to feel a sense of genuine happiness and peace like she did. I remember someone in treatment telling me early on, "Roxanne, what would you do if you were trying to start a relationship with anybody? You would talk to them, spend time with them and learn about them, right? So that's all you have to do". And that's how it started for me. I would talk to Him by praying, spending time with Him by starting to meditate and learn about Him by reading His word and talking to other women there that believed in God and had their own personal relationships with Him; mainly this woman I just told you of. Before long we both ended up on laundry duty together and spent several hours a day together, just her and I folding clothes and talking. I was able to ask her questions. I would have felt stupid asking anyone else but was able to talk freely to her and explore this new relationship in my life. From there it has grown and continues to grow daily. I think it is important that I believe in my understanding of God and value my personal relationship with Him. Had I not been willing to open that door and develop my own concept and understanding of God, I never would have had the relationship I have with Him today, and it is beyond what I imagined I wanted initially. Again, I don't believe I would still be sober, or for that matter alive today had I not been willing to do that.

I had many ups and downs and "Ah-Ha" moments while in treatment. There was another woman that was very special during that part of my journey. She was honest, brutally so, but in a non-confrontational way. You could see she was genuine, could relate to you without judgement and basically loved you enough to tell you the truth instead of what you wanted to hear, and I needed that. Because of my personality and height, not many women had been willing to do that with me in the past. I scared or intimidated them, but not her. I later found out she too lost her husband suddenly, so again I believed God placed her in my life, so I would be able to talk to someone who I believed understood how I felt and what I was going through. Treatment is simple but far from easy; you have to be willing to be uncomfortable. I tell people if you are comfortable, you're not growing……push yourself; you get out what you put in.

About two weeks after I arrived in treatment I got two angry letters from my parents a couple of days in a row. The reality of my actions and the destruction I had caused was settling in and they were having to deal with the wreckage I left behind. When I first got to treatment, I would see other women crying when sharing and although I was feeling emotions again, I couldn't cry at first. I feared that maybe I was broken or something, but that was just the effects of going numb for so long; it takes time. Well, after getting the letter from my mother and then the following day one from my father where they laid into me about everything, I went out to a gazebo by myself and cried for over an hour straight. It was like once I started I couldn't stop, and I hated it. I was so angry, but really at myself, my situation and my reality. My head had cleared enough at this point to where I looked around and thought, "Dammit Roxanne, look at where you are, and what you have done to your life and kids……again!" I felt like my parents no longer considered me a part of the family and had tricked me into going to treatment and just pretended to be supportive to get me there and was convinced they were going to try to take my kids from me legally and got myself all worked up. The problem wasn't them or anything they were doing, they were helping me, but at the time I was so angry with myself and my situation, that was how I was thinking. Of course, that wasn't the case. They were just angry and rightfully so.

For the first few months I was in treatment, the man that had been living with me and I still wrote each other almost every day. I still thought I was "in love" and would actually tell people, "We're engaged, the ring is just still in the pawn shop". Which was true, because we pawned that ring, that his mother paid for, for dope multiple times, and somehow in my mind that was a symbol of love. Initially I would get letters where he talked about meetings and his sponsor, etc. and after some time the letters became fewer until they eventually stopped altogether. At one point he did make it back into a treatment, I know because he attempted to write me a letter from there, which was intercepted due to being against the rules to write from one treatment center or jail to another. However, I later learned that he stayed there barely a week before being kicked out due to sneaking pills into the treatment center. I had this strange sense that I can only compare to what I have heard others describe as survivor's guilt. Because I was sober and getting better, I felt guilty that he had not and wanted him to be able to be better also. But I know better than anybody that NO ONE can want it or do it for you. The truth is he had every opportunity to get the help he needed just like I did, he just didn't choose to change. And after I started working a program and learning to love myself I saw our relationship for what it was, not love, just my understanding of what love was at that time. He is sick, and I pray that he is able to get well, but I know today that it isn't my job to help him; I can't help him. That isn't me being heartless, that's me loving myself. Our relationship was codependent, unhealthy and centered on destructive behaviors and thinking. I know today that he would be able to get me high before I could get him sober, and I love myself and my loved ones enough to protect my sobriety today.

I remember after I had been in treatment several months and was beginning to progress in my thinking, my faith and learning to love myself while dealing with life on life's terms, having a conversation with our manager; someone I love dearly and still consider a friend to this day. I asked her on a long drive where we were alone, "What good man is ever going to really want me? I'm a widow with two young children, I have a history of sexual trauma and physical abuse, I have been to treatment multiple times and am an alcoholic and IV heroin addict….". I didn't feel worthy of a "healthy", "normal", relationship, and didn't think a "good" man would ever see me as anything but those things. She simply looked at me and said, "Oh Roxanne…..you are such a beautiful person and soul. You deserve the best in life, and I know you can't see it now, but if you continue to work and do as you have been, God will bring you someone that is worthy of you and your love…..and he will be lucky to have you". I remember tearing up, I wanted to believe her even though I couldn't really yet. And she had been one of the first people to see beauty and strength in me in a very long time; I wasn't comfortable being complimented. She probably doesn't even remember that conversation, but it meant so much to me and still does. That reinforces to me that we can impact people without ever knowing it, and to always show love in our actions with others. It can make a life changing difference for someone; I know because others have done that for me.

    I remember as I neared the end of my six months in treatment feeling a little scared of the challenges going home would bring, but proud of myself. And I should be proud, but not entitled. There was a part of me that thought that my hometown should have a parade waiting for me when I arrived home, because they had no idea how hard it was for me to achieve being six months sober. But, really, I was doing what I should have been doing all along, and what people do every day because that is life and they don't expect an award for it. When my parents and children came to my final visitation before I completed treatment they pulled up in a brand-new vehicle. I was so excited. My truck had been repossessed my second week of treatment and I did not have a car to drive once I got home. I said to myself, "Yes! Roxanne got a new truck for completing treatment!!". I practically sang it in my head and did a little happy dance. So even six months sober, my thinking was still entitled and selfish. That wasn't my new truck, it was my mother's new truck. However, after I returned home my father provided me an option of using my tax return to purchase her old truck from him and I did. I paid for insurance on it and went to get a new tag and when he signed the title over to me I added a stipulation to the title that, although it was in my name, it could not be title pawned without my father's signature. That wasn't him making me do anything because he didn't trust me, that was me attempting to build trust and be transparent rather than defensive because he deserved that from me.

    Once I got home from treatment I was terrified, I didn't want to mess up and had a bunch of tools I had learned, but now I had to implement them, figure out was what going to work for me and what wasn't, and make my recovery mine. Again, you get out of it what you put into it and this is something I had never done in the past. Initially my parents were afraid too and very watchful, but eventually started trying to trust me more and more and allow me more freedom, because deep down they knew if I wanted to drink or use they couldn't stop that from happening, but they also wanted me to be successful. I can clearly recall the first time I was driving alone without my kids or anyone else and, out of nowhere, I had the thought, "I could use right now, and no one would know it, and it would be cheap; I don't have a tolerance anymore". Now after ALL that I had been through to get to where I was, any logical person would ask, "Are you CRAZY?!?! Have you lost your mind??? Why in the world would you think like that, are you INSANE???"; no, I'm an addict. And I have learned that even the person with the strongest recovery in the room at some point had sick thinking and that thought is normal; it's what I do with it today that is different. So, I picked up the phone and called my sponsor. When I said it out loud, I heard how crazy it sounded and it lost power. I wasn't obsessing about it and letting it become a plan in my mind. We relapse in our minds and thinking long before we ever pick up a drink or drug. And all she had to say to me was, "Roxanne…..you would know". And she was right, so I took myself to a meeting and didn't use. I made a choice that day. I tell people all the time that yes, "I have a disease, but that isn't an excuse for my actions and today I have a choice. Today I am not in active addiction. My disease DEMANDS to be treated every day. I can choose to treat it with recovery or I will eventually treat it by using, but every day I have a choice".

I did things that made me uncomfortable because people that had long term sobriety and had happy lives suggested I should, if I wanted what they had too. I became engaged in a 12-step program and actively applied spiritual principles in my everyday life; I allowed others to love me until I loved myself, I learned how to feel validated from within rather than from men or other external sources, I was privileged to be able to be a mother to my boys rather than taking their love for granted. In sobriety life has not always been easy; life still shows up: I had to go back and testify against my abuser in a second trial, my brother passed away, I have faced challenges due to my actions and consequences while in active addiction, but I managed all of those things sober and am genuinely happy today for the first time in my life. Today I have a sense of peace I have never known. I remember being at my son's 13th birthday party sitting around a fire at the lake when I first really noticed and appreciated it. I was almost a year sober and was able just to "be" and be happy. I wasn't faking anything; my mind wasn't racing with how to come up with an excuse to run to the gas station and get away from everyone long enough to get a fix. I was just fully present, at peace and content. There is no better gift I have ever been given. Today I am in a healthy and loving relationship with a man I adore. He is not in recovery, however knows every bit of my story and who I am and loves me more for it. He sees strength and beauty in my scars and what I have overcome, rather than having pity or judgement. I know the difference today between intimacy and sex, I know how to fully trust and love someone and feel worthy of them loving and trusting me too. I learned how to let someone love me. My children are happy, they are well adjusted and proud of my recovery today. My parents sleep easy at night again and share my story hoping to give others hope today rather than being ashamed of my past. I am truly blessed and grateful for the life I have today.

If there is one thing I could ask that people take away from my story is that it is WORTH it and there is HOPE (HOPE=Hold On Pain Ends). If I could just let you feel how good the feeling I have today is, you would see that it is better than anything you can possibly imagine early on and worth ALL of it. I know, especially early on that I did not believe that I could have the things I heard others talk about gaining in their sobriety. I thought I was different, didn't deserve it, and would fail again. So, know that I understand if you don't believe that right now, but BELIEVE THAT I BELIEVE, and for right now, that's enough. We CAN and DO recover!

The Bridges of Hope, Alamo, GA. This is where I was blessed to attend treatment and learn how to not only GET sober, but STAY sober! I can never express enough gratitude for the B.O.H

Chapter 2

Finding Rock Bottom

It's not a challenge....it's surrender

I've heard many people talk about what motivated them to get clean and sober. My experience was not some epiphany or desire to change my life. Simply put I was out of options and the pain and insanity I was sitting in was worse than my fear of admitting I needed help in that moment. I rolled over and groaned when the consciousness of my reality came into focus. I immediately smell myself...I hadn't showered in days, my teeth felt fuzzy, I reeked of body odor and my first thought was *I need heroin, how can I get some, how can I pay for it, who might front me again?* I laid still not having the energy to open my eyes, my arms felt impossibly heavy and I was so angry…. angry at my situation, at myself for this being my reality….just angry, at everything. I looked towards the window trying to determine the time of day, so I could begin to formulate a plan. At this point of my addiction I didn't sleep in a traditional way or during the conventional times. I would pass or nod out periodically and whenever the substance I was using starting to wear off my body would respond by waking me up to get more. It is ALL I cared about, above anything else – stop the pain, go numb…..survive. Which is ironic really because I was apathetic about dying – I really was just too afraid to feel the pain.

I slowly opened my eyes and could see light – the clock read 6:00 – I had to stop and think AM or PM? By the light in the window it could really be either, I honestly couldn't tell. I was absolutely miserable. Using was no longer optional, even if I didn't want to use, I had to. If I didn't use I became so "dope sick" that I couldn't function. It usually started with my nose running, my eyes would begin to water, I would start sweating, then came the pain in my stomach and legs, running to the bathroom with explosive diarrhea and vomiting at the same time. Mind you, if someone called and had what I needed I somehow would muster up the energy to get to them. I even carried the vomit bags they give you at the ER (I had collected several since I frequented the ER those days) in the door of my car so I could throw up at red lights in route to get more drugs. I would sit up at night and see commercials advertising various treatment centers and would want to go but felt like I couldn't. I had been to detox several times and treatment once in the past, that my parents had to pay out of pocket for, since I had quit working long before and no longer had health insurance. When I completed my first treatment I was threatened and warned by my parents that relapse was "not an option" for me and they would move to take custody of my children if I ever used again, so I was afraid to admit to them where I was in my addiction and what my and my children's reality had become. Anyone that is an addict or alcoholic can tell you though, that no amount of love or threats will keep you from using very long without some sort of treatment or program, as much as I wished it were possible, the compulsion and need to use and drink overpowered my ability to reason rationally. So there I was…..hopeless.

I started this chapter by saying rock bottom is surrender rather than a challenge. That might sound weird initially, however I experienced many people in recovery judging others "bottoms" and almost having pride for going lower -- almost like it became a contest to some, who was a "worse" addict or alcoholic than another. Early on I admit that at times I was guilty of this myself, almost bragging when I would tell others that I was a "low bottom user". Seriously???? Yes, seriously. That is a perfect example of the insanity of my thinking.

My self-esteem had become so non-existent that the one thing I had pride for was that I was good at being a "fuck up", like I was a "good addict". Is there really such a thing? Like when word spread around about someone overdosing, rather than being overcome with fear or empathy I wanted to find out where they got their dope, because to me that meant it was good, strong dope, and I was "smart enough" to do it right and not kill myself. INSANE THINKING. Like someone I love, and respect says all the time, it isn't your drinking or using that got you to your bottom, it was your thinking. Not only was I demeaning myself, I was belittling people, who had stopped before getting to the point I had and realized they needed help, minimizing the validity of their feelings when sharing their experience in an effort to get better. Like somehow their story and pain was less valid than mine? Or even sadly providing them the ammunition they needed to rationalize that maybe they could use or drink "successfully" because they weren't as bad as me, something else I have been guilty of. I was that girl in my first treatment center that called my dad and told him I didn't belong there, with "those people". Yes, I had a problem with drinking but there were heroin addicts there, I didn't need to be around, "people like that". By the time I arrived at my last treatment center I had become the very girl I judged previously; an IV heroin addict.

It doesn't matter if you just drink, just drug, are a heroin addict, a meth addict, an IV user or not…..all of it gets you to the same place eventually, some just faster than others. We all get to a point where our lives have become unmanageable and the discomfort of continuing to use and/or drink becomes worse than the fear of quitting and facing our reality, which in my case included all of the feelings and emotions I ran from and numbed myself from for years. In recovery this is called the "jumping off point", where you are provided with "the gift of desperation". Although it didn't feel much like a gift to me at the time. Using and drinking had stopped working long ago and like I said earlier, I used just to avoid being deathly ill; anything on top of that was a rare bonus at that point. So, any rational person would ask, well why in the world wouldn't you just stop then?

I can remember my mom looking at me in disbelief and confusion saying, "Roxanne, I know you love your boys more than anything in this world, why can't you just stop?!?!" The sad part is deep down I wanted to, I just couldn't. It made me feel even more hopeless. I knew how much I loved them and they meant to me and if that was not enough to make me stop I didn't think I'd ever be able to. I had become so ashamed of myself and felt like a complete failure.

There are two quotes that I always liked and hit home for me about hitting rock bottom. The first is from recovery literature and states that "rock bottom is when you stop digging" (AA Big Book, p.325), and another from JK Rowling that states "Rock bottom became the solid foundation on which I rebuilt my life". And really that is what rock bottom is, and why it is different for everyone. You can stop and begin to rebuild at any point. By listening to other's bottoms, it is not to compare or validate my own experience, it is simply to have gratitude for my life in recovery today and learn from their experience, because I know if I haven't already experienced the things they have, if I remain in active addiction, at some point I will. It just may or may not have happened……YET. It reinforces for me that this disease does not discriminate, and so many others have felt the way I have and tried to manage to continue to drink and use successfully and inevitably had the same outcome. The definition of insanity is doing the same thing over and over and expecting a different result. By listening to other's stories and bottoms I am able to believe that there is no such thing as using successfully for an addict or alcoholic, so there is no point in continuing to try.

The hardest part of hitting rock bottom for me was admitting that I had, and surrendering to the fact that now, if I wanted to get better I HAD to do something about it. There has never been anything else in my life that, if I wanted it badly enough and tried hard enough, I could not achieve…..until this. It took some time for me to realize that this surrender was not giving up, it was a start to a new life. I do see that moment of clarity as a gift today. Like Rowling's quote, that is where I was finally able to start rebuilding my life with a solid foundation, really for the first time. If I had not gone through what I did and experienced the things I have, I don't believe I would be where I am today or appreciate my life for what it is today. Even at my sickest when my thinking was completely irrational, I was blessed to have a moment of clarity and insight that allowed me to get out of my own way and start to get better.

As I sat in the middle of nowhere Georgia, sore from being sober, and having to work and participate in treatment for a couple of weeks, I thought to myself, "Now what Roxanne? Look at what you have done and where you are…..how did you let things get so out of control?". I wondered where my "boyfriend/fiancée" was and if he was sober and miserable too. It's not that I didn't understand or know that what I was doing was wrong, or didn't, on some level want to stop and change. I honestly just didn't think it was worth it. "If I'm going to be miserable anyway, why go through all this? If I'm using at least I can go numb from feeling this way and maybe it will all just be over sooner". "What do sober people do for fun?" "Who would want to date me now, knowing not only am I a single widowed mother of two, but also an alcoholic and drug addict. Hell, not just a drug addict but an IV heroin addict?!?!" "What if I really try and give it all I can and still fail?". There was a part of me that knew I wasn't completely bought into changing when I was in treatment in the past, and was simply taking a break, so I didn't feel as bad when I relapsed because a part of me always expected to. So, if I bought in completely and gave this all I had, and failed, then I knew I would be a lost cause. I was held paralyzed by fear of failure because I had never been able to be successful in maintaining my sobriety in the past. If I really started to change and failed again I knew deep down that my family would give up on me, and once I started getting better there had always been pressure and expectations along with that. I remember thinking, "What happened to you just wanting me to stop using?". My sick thinking would reinforce my wanting to give up; telling me that when I'm using people just see me as a junkie and don't expect anything from me, so at least that way I'm not letting anyone down. It is ABSOLUTELY crazy thinking when I look back on it, but that is how my brain operated at that time. In fact, this is how it is for most, if not all addicts I have talked to in early recovery.

The shift in thinking started when I stopped looking at rock bottom as the end, and instead looked at my bottom as my new beginning and an opportunity to get my life back. When I was early on in treatment I remember having a group where I was asked to write a "goodbye/chump" letter to my drug of choice (heroin). As if I were breaking up with a boyfriend and ending a relationship. This sounded a bit absurd to me initially, but I gained insight and perspective while completing this exercise. Prior to doing this I viewed drugs and alcohol as something I used, not something I was in a relationship with. But the reality was that I was in a very unhealthy and codependent relationship with a substance. I had made heroin my everything, it was my "God" and Higher Power, it was my significant other, my best friend and what I turned to when I was happy, sad, lonely and hurt. In active addiction I was in a "relationship" with a substance! I put it above my children, my family, my friends, my life. And now I had to tell it goodbye. It was almost like I was grieving the loss. That sounds insane to someone that is not an addict or alcoholic I'm sure, "Why wouldn't you be happy to be rid of something that caused you so much harm and destruction in your life?", but that's how I felt. I fondly remember an old timer (someone with several years of sobriety) telling me, "We act like we're giving up something good!" and he was right. We desperately try to hold on to the very thing that is killing us and causing us so much pain. I don't have a copy of the original letter I wrote that day; after reading it to a peer of mine, I burned it in a bonfire meeting while in treatment to have a tangible way to say goodbye to my addiction and begin to move forward. I did however find a copy of the poem/handout a friend gave me before we completed the exercise. It is typical for addicts to "romanticize their using and addiction, remember the "good times" rather than all of the pain and consequences. So, she provided me a letter from my "love", my drug of choice, heroin. I included the letter from heroin below for you…..even if you are not a heroin addict (like I said I finally realized ANYTHING that changed the way I felt I would abuse), you can easily substitute your drink or drug of choice and it will still be fitting. After reading this, ask yourself if this is a friend or love that you want to keep in your life. After reading this, take a moment and ask yourself…….What might your letter look like?

I am Heroin:

I destroy homes, tear families apart, take your children, and that's just the start. I'm more costly than diamonds, more costly than gold, the sorrow I bring is a sight to behold, and if you need me, I'm so easily found. I live all around you, and hang out in town. I live with the rich, I live with the poor, I live down the street, and might be next door. My power is awesome; test me you'll see. But if you do, you may never break free! Just try me once and

I might let you go, but try me twice, and I'll own your soul. When I possess you, you'll steal and you'll lie. You'll do what you have to just to get high. The crimes you'll commit, for my narcotic name, to you it's worth the pleasure of me in your veins. You'll lie to your Mother; you'll steal from your Dad. When you see their tears, you should feel sad. But you'll forget your morals and how you were raised, I'll take over your conscience, and shorten your days. I take kids from parents, and parents from kids, I turn people from God, and separate from friends. I'll take everything from you, from your looks to your pride, I'll be with you always, right by your side. You'll give up everything - your family, your home, your friends, your money, you'll be mine and mine alone!!!! I'll take and take, till you have nothing more to give, when I'm finished with you, you'll be lucky to live. If you try me be warned - this is no game, if given the chance, I'll drive you insane. I'll ravish your body; I'll control your mind, I'll own you completely; your soul will be mine! The nightmares I'll give you while lying in bed, the voices you'll hear from inside your head. The sweats, the shakes, the visions you'll see, I want you to know, these are all part of the poison of me. I'll strip you of faith and be your only love, you lose all hope, I'll be all you think of. You'll regret that you tried me, they always do, but you came to me, not I to you!! You knew this would happen, many times you were told, but you challenged my power, and chose to be bold. You could have said no, and just walked away, if you could live that day over, now what would you say? I'll be your master; you will be my slave, I'll even go with you, when you go to your grave. Now that you have me, what will you do? Will you try me or not, it's all up to you. I will bring you more misery than words can tell, if you take my hand, I'll drag you to hell!

- Author Unknown

It was important for me in my recovery journey to gain insight into how I had let the chaos I had been living in, while in active addiction, become my new "normal" for lack of a better term. I was comfortable with the chaos, it was familiar. Even if I knew all of the bad things that came along with it, that was where I was comfortable, and things didn't seem crazy or insane to me anymore.

I would go back to using and what I knew in that lifestyle, not because I thought things would be better, but it was a "familiar misery", where I knew what to expect. The fear of failure and the unknown would become uncomfortable, so I would turn back to a comfort zone of chaos, like I was uncomfortable with things just being on an even keel. I have heard many other addicts relate to that feeling, but early on we don't realize that is what we are doing. When things get good or start to normalize we get uncomfortable since we have made the chaotic lifestyle we had in active addiction become our "new normal". Once we become uncomfortable we create chaos in our lives and start to self-sabotage, usually subconsciously. Once I was able to look at this pattern in my behavior objectively and honestly, with a sober mind I was able to start to respond rather than react and change my behavior. I was able to accept I was at rock bottom, see that it was an opportunity and become WILLING to change. I tell people all the time that if you are comfortable you aren't growing. Push yourself out of your comfort zone and allow yourself to grow, it's worth it. I had to shift my thinking early on. It wasn't about, "Not having anything to lose", losing things stopped mattering to me in active addiction. It was about, "What I had to gain in sobriety", and realizing that even though I didn't see it at that time, I could be happy in sobriety, and I was worthy of that happiness.

If you are reading this book and in the beginning of your journey, or someone that has been sober for a while and questioning if you have really reached your bottom and can try just one more time……STOP DIGGING! If you are reading this, most likely you are already there, you don't HAVE to keep going and you shouldn't. The truth is that I know I have another run in me, but I don't believe I have another recovery in me so it's not worth it today. I don't think I would make it back again, and today I don't want to die. I am genuinely happy with my life just the way it is and comfortable in my own skin, and with who I am today. The consequences aren't worth it anymore, and I am forever grateful.

Chapter 3

Being in Treatment - The Beginning

You Get Out What You Put In....

I have been to more than one inpatient treatment center and since getting sober have been fortunate enough to work in a couple of residential treatment centers as well. All of them were very different than each other in many ways, but one thing is always the same.....the addicts and alcoholics. Our thinking, our actions, our challenges early on are very consistent from environment to environment. We're survivors, we adapt, we evaluate our situation and manipulate it to benefit us and create our own version of a best case scenario to get through the situation we find ourselves in…..it's instinct and I have done it myself and witnessed others doing the same. I came from a reality where I didn't trust anyone and didn't believe that anyone had genuine motives, because that is how I thought and was, so I assumed other people were the same and "faking". I remember being somewhat relieved and offended at the same time when a woman I was in treatment with called me out on what I was doing and simply told me, "Roxanne, you don't have to live like that anymore"…… and thank goodness she was right.

    I sat in a chair against a wall, I preferred my back to the wall, it was a way of living and defense mechanism I didn't even consciously know I had started doing, just a product of the lifestyle I had been living and making sure no one could approach me without me knowing or catching me off-guard. I started to observe the activity and people around me. There were about 40 women living at this facility at the time I arrived, and I was so used to being isolated I looked around at my home for the next 6 months overwhelmed, it seemed like chaos. But as naturally as breathing comes to me, I started evaluating the situation. Who seemed fake? Who was in charge? Who did everyone listen to? Who did I think I would like/dislike? Who do I need to make my friend here to make this as painless as possible? I can remember thinking "Ugh…." not because I had created such destruction in my love ones lives and was putting my children through this again, no my thinking was still too selfish then for that. I was thinking "Ugh" because I looked around and was disgusted at the thought of having to live with and get along with so many women. I viewed all women as being "catty" and "emotional", full of drama and I could only imagine the disagreements and middle school behavior that would start to surface surrounded by so many women. Of course, I didn't realize or acknowledge at that time, my frustration was really that I would have to learn how to manage conflict, be less selfish, and build genuine relationships rather than turn to a man for validation, as recovery literature states, "the easier, softer way" (AA Big Book, p.58).

I started to learn the way the facility operated and the authority structure. Found the women that I thought were similar to me and my way of thinking, etc. And even with all that I had done and been through I STILL caught myself thinking I was better than to cope with my own actions. I looked around and realized about 90% of the women there were mandated to treatment due to legal problems or had served time in jail or prison at some point and I remember thinking, "Well, at least I was never arrested". I realized pretty quickly how insane this thinking was. In speaking to the women, I realized I had committed almost ALL of the same crimes throughout my active addiction, the only difference is that I had not been caught. I was no better or worse than any of those women, we were all sick, all of our lives had become unmanageable and we were all there because we needed to learn how to STAY and LIVE sober and get our lives back.

I can remember after being at treatment about two weeks and having a moment where I was sitting alone and thought to myself, "Look where you are. I can't believe I've done this....again to my family......my poor boys.....and I've messed up even worse this time......now what? What am I going to do? Can I come back from this......or is this just hopeless??" I was so full of shame I couldn't look myself in the eye when brushing my teeth. The person I had become in active addiction was something that I was overwhelmingly ashamed of, and now sitting with my consequences and reality slapping me in my face without a substance to use to run from my feelings; I just felt hopeless.

I was angry about all of the rules (under 30 days of being there you had additional rules), I was angry that I was in a bunk bed for the first time in my life at 34 years old, I was angry that I HAD to do things that I didn't want to....work, meetings, readings, devotions, prayers......I aimed my anger at my situation rather than myself. But the truth was I was just so angry at myself because of what I had allowed my life to become. I was angry long before I stopped using if I'm to be honest. I would see people walking in the grocery store or down a sidewalk and would be angry at them, just because they seemed happy. I had gotten to a place of being angry at happy people because I was so unhappy and jealous that they had something I found unattainable for myself.

So, I started going through the motions, doing what I had to do, without getting kicked out. I knew I had no options but to stay so I had no choice, which today I am so grateful for, because had I been given an out I would have taken it, and I truly believe I would be dead today. I couldn't sleep at all in the beginning. My body ached, my legs were killing me, I caught a cold because my immune system was nonexistent. I was thin and frail, but finally had an appetite but didn't like most of what was served and was hungry. I would lay in bed at night staring at the ceiling listening to one of my roommates' snore and the other moan and cry out due to her nightmares. I was miserable, and rather than being present in my thoughts they were consumed with where my "fiancé" was and what he was doing. "Was he still sober too? Why hasn't he written me yet?" So, I would sit and write him letters, mailing them out every day. We could only send two letters a day, and my thinking was still so misguided, I would write him every day and then alternate a letter to my boys and then one to my parents every other day or try to put multiple letters in one envelope to make sure I could still write him too.

After a couple of weeks, the letters started coming for me too. I got mail almost every day. My mom sent me a package with items I "needed" once she realized I was actually going to stay but made a point to use the money from my bank account to reinforce I was on my own financially now. I remember making a list of things I "needed" to send home to my parents and before I knew it the list had become very long and filled a sheet of paper front and back. That is when a peer of mine that had been there in treatment multiple months now talked to me about the difference between needs and wants. How I needed to balance rather than being selfish. She pointed out that I had listed things like hair color when less than a month ago I wasn't even regularly showering or washing my hair…….she gave me much needed perspective because my thinking was still so impulsive and self-focused. I started a new list…..and needless to say it became much shorter.

The letters from my parents initially were very supportive. They were reassuring me that my boys were ok, and they were not concerned with the past; that they just wanted me to start over and build a new future and be able to be a mother again. They were encouraging me to stay in treatment and try to finally get better this time…..they were grateful I was there and terrified of what the future would hold as they started to accept the fact that they were powerless over my addiction as well. But the tone changed after a couple of weeks when the reality of the situation hit and the relief of me being safe subsided. I started getting a few angry letters where they were venting about all I had done to them and my boys throughout active addiction. They had started going thru and attempting to clean up my home and found things that blew their minds (drug paraphernalia, actual drugs, empty closets from everything being sold or pawned, and just the amount of filth we were living in). That is when I cried for the first time since being in treatment. I felt bad and thought maybe I was broken the first few weeks. I would be in groups and meetings and feel emotional but couldn't cry and didn't understand - I thought maybe I really had become dead inside. But the truth was that I had been going numb with heroin for so long it took time for me to heal enough to be able to. But once it hit I felt like I couldn't stop, like a dam had broken open and I was overwhelmed with emotions that had become so foreign to me. I hated it, I was so uncomfortable. But I now know when you are uncomfortable that it when growth happens, you have to go through it to get to the other side. If you are comfortable in rehab, start working -- if you're comfortable you're not actively working on a life of recovery; you are taking a break until your next run…..that's just the honest truth. So, if you are in treatment and reading this, ask yourself, "How comfortable am I? Why or why not?" and then get motivated to make a change. Yes it can be painful, but it's worth it and the alternative is much more painful, if you haven't already learned that for yourself…..trust me, I did the research for you and learned the hard way.

I remember being angry at and resenting my Mom in the beginning for "taking my kids from me". But the reality was I gave them away. I took being a mother for granted during active addiction rather than seeing it as a privilege like I do today. It was a big dose of humility for me and when my perspective and thinking started to change, when I got a letter from my Mom one day with my boys reports cards included. She talked about all the activities they were involved in at church and school and for the holidays and both their grades had gone up. It was a difficult feeling; my pride was hurt because I had evidence in front of me that my actions had a negative impact on my kids and could not live in denial anymore. I was happy that they were doing better and thriving because I love them, and I am their mother, but at the same time I was hurt and humbled by the fact that I had to be removed from them for them to get better; that I was the problem. And that was the beginning of my thinking shifting from anger and resentment towards my mother to gratitude for her and my father being able to take care of my kids when I could not and having somewhere where they could be safe and loved while I was given an opportunity to get better -- yes I actually saw treatment as an opportunity at that point rather than a punishment, but it took time. Time for my brain to heal, time to start to learn from the women around me……much needed time.

I remember having a meeting in treatment where I was told, "Addiction is a family disease….. one person may use, but the whole family suffers". I had been playing the victim of my circumstances for so long and was so self-focused on what I had been through that I hadn't even thought of the true impact my illness brought on my family who didn't ask for this. I saw they were on an emotional roller coaster and trying to heal just like me when reading their letters. I would get one that was hopeful, happy and supportive. Excerpt from a letter from my Mom on 11/18/14 (40 days sober) following my first family visitation: "We all enjoyed our visit with you on Sunday. It did all of us good to lay eyes on you and see the place where you're spending this time. Especially the boys. They were both so happy to see you. You look good. Keep up the hard work and learn once and for good how to beat this". **Excerpt from a letter from my Dad on 10/15/14 (5 days sober):** "It will take work on both of us to get things where they need to be, but I KNOW WE CAN. The boys need their mother back. You do your part and we will do ours and six months from now we can be a real family again. I love you and always will". **Then, I would get another where they were afraid and questioning things that were said or done and so full of fear I would describe them as being cautiously optimistic. Excerpt from a letter from my Mom on 12/9/14 (61 days sober)** "Not sure if you will get this before Sunday, our next visit, but I had the urge to write. I've had a "feeling" about you since seeing you last

Sunday; A couple of dreams also. We all need to remain completely honest with each other. There is too much at stake not to be. Was there another elephant in the room?"

Excerpt from a letter from my Dad on 10/25/14 (15 days sober): "We got your letter today and I am very proud of the things you are saying. You have to understand that you have not told the truth in the past and trust will be an issue we will have to work on together. You spoke of your first visitation and we are planning on being there with the kids because we all know how much it will mean to you and we miss you too! You spoke of how you would understand if we did not come every weekend so as not to take up every Sunday.

The Dad in me thinks WOW! After only two weeks Roxanne is trying to be considerate of others! But the new prove it Dad has to think is that because you would tell your boyfriend to come visit if you know we are not coming?" **And finally, I'd get letters full of anger or hurt feelings, sometimes outright rage. Excerpt from a letter from my Mom on 10/27/14 (17 days sober):** "I've had quite the drug use awareness program from cleaning the home where you were supposed to be raising your children. I have washed walls and cleaned sinks, toilets and showers of some brown looking stuff I assume was the heroin. I've swept and vacuumed hundreds of tiny little bags, pieces of what I guess were syringes, tin foil, etc. I remember you asking me for potting soil, so you could plant some flowers out front - I am/was so stupid! I saw what you were growing on the balcony off your bedroom.... (a marijuana plant) I'm not trying to be mean, but I don't have meetings to go to, so I can get out my frustrations and snap out of it. I'm busy running your life and raising your children because you couldn't, while you are off getting better." **An excerpt from a letter**

from my Dad on 11/16/14 (38 days sober) "My vision for our future: Me your mother and your boys are going to have a clean and safe home and be a family. When you come home, me and your mom will help and when you get a good job and prove to ALL of us you are going to stay clean and sober we will begin to trust you again. None of my vision includes another man to be a part of your sons lives that you said you would never put anything ahead of again. It's going to be hard enough for all of us to forgive you. Things that happened in this house and in front of the boys will NEVER happen again. I love you very much, but I am very serious about your and the boys future".

As you can see from the real examples of the letters I received from my parents while I was in treatment, my disease of addiction had my family just as sick as me, when they didn't deserve it. Throughout addiction we "retrain" our families on how to communicate and interact with us without even realizing it. They lie for us, they enable us due to their love for us being manipulated, they fight with each other out of frustration and fear…..all while I had allowed denial to convince me that, "I was only hurting myself". By keeping and reading these letters back from early on in my recovery I can see that they were healing too. They even acknowledged it themselves in letters to me. Excerpt from a letter from my Mom on 11/23/14 (45 days sober): *"Just like you are on a journey to recovery, in a way all the rest of us are also. Our love for you, and only you and the boys, is the only thing that keeps me and Dad sane enough to do this".* **An excerpt from a letter from my Dad on 10/29/14 (19 days sober):** *"Your last letter from me may have been a little rough but I needed to make sure you know how I feel. Please understand me and your Mom are working thru issues of anger and changes as well as you are".* **The letters from my boys consistently told me how much they loved and missed me as well as how much they were looking forward to me coming home and having a "normal family again". They desperately just wanted their mother back.**

Something else that I have reflected back on throughout my recovery and helped me tremendously while in treatment was journaling. I have learned in recovery that simply sharing something with someone and saying it out loud in itself helps. It takes power away from my negative thoughts rather than letting them sit and become a plan or something that impacts me emotionally. Typically, by the time I finish saying it I can hear and realize how insane my thinking sounds. Well early on I didn't trust anyone else to say my thoughts out loud to yet, so journaling and writing them down helped me to get them out of my head and reading them back I could begin to see I was thinking irrationally at times. When I was faced with difficult things in life (life on life's terms) I can go back and see a drastic difference in my thinking, reasoning and coping skills. I came across a good example of this from an entry I made on 2/23/15 (a little more than 4 months sober): "My thoughts have been all over the map the last couple of days. I am in a really good place spiritually right now; however, I have been very emotional about past memories, issues and relationships that have been on my mind. It caught me off guard honestly - but I am trying to let myself feel my emotions, go thru them and move forward rather than dwell. I believe God is putting these things in my mind right now for a reason and so I can face and address them while I am still here in a "safe" and supportive environment. My relationship with God helps me to find and be at peace. I cannot control what thoughts I have - HOWEVER I now CAN control how I deal with and act on those thoughts. That is a relief and empowering!" **I was able to process my thoughts and emotions then much more than four months prior and can see I was relying on a power greater than myself, which I adamantly didn't buy into prior to coming to treatment this time. I'm still in awe of the extreme differences in my thinking in just four months' time.**

I also received letters from the boyfriend/fiancé/drug buddy that I was living with in an unhealthy and codependent relationship when I left for treatment. Pretty much daily or every other day once they started arriving for almost 3 months into my treatment. He wrote with an element of panic and desperation due to feeling like he had lost his ability to influence me, know what I was thinking and doing, etc. He would repeatedly tell me how much he loved me, that we were meant to be together, that he was afraid and wanting me to promise and reassure him that I would not "get sober and decide to leave him". I know now, that he knew if I were well I wouldn't be ok with our relationship the way it was, and he didn't think he could change. It was more comfortable for him if I stayed sick, because then he didn't feel threatened with losing me. He would sign them "Your future husband...." which made me feel a sense of pressure to remain loyal to him, which conflicted with everything I was learning about myself, a life of recovery and what my children and family deserved from me.

When the letters abruptly stopped I assumed he had relapsed but convinced myself that if he were able he would still write me and let me know he was ok, our love was "too strong" for me to believe he would just stop communicating with me. I remember telling another woman in treatment with me, "I know him. He must be in jail or dead from an overdose. There is no way he wouldn't write me if he could". After being in treatment for a little more than 90 days I was able to go on my first pass and learned that I was wrong. I got a much needed reality check. Addiction is addiction. What we had wasn't really love, but I had to be removed from it long enough to be able to view it objectively. He was alive and free, he was just using again and stopped writing me. Of course when he had an opportunity to speak to me, he played the martyr and told me that, "He wasn't using, just selling" and when I was able to see right through what he was saying he told me, "He loved me too much to continue writing me while he was messing up, he felt guilty and didn't want to pull me down because he was proud I was doing so good". Right before he asked if I could meet him somewhere, because he still didn't have a license or car and "just wanted to talk". Thank goodness I was surrounded by support and family and had learned enough to look at what is important to me and who truly loved me, had been there for me and needed me and I came to terms with what our relationship really was and ended any additional contact with him. For a bit I felt guilty, like a sense of survivor's guilt because I got well, and he was still sick. But he had every opportunity that I did to get treatment and get well and chose not to take it. My loyalty was now to my kids, my sobriety and my family. I knew in my heart if he needed help, he could get it without my involvement, he knew how, and I also now could admit to myself that he would get me high again before I could get him sober, I just had to practice

acceptance - it was what it was.

Chapter 4

Being in Treatment - Building my Foundation

Am I Ready to go Home...???

I can remember thinking, "I've got this". I had been in treatment for a few months now. I was feeling good physically again, able to sleep through the night and even grab a nap some days when we had time in our schedule. I had gained weight, about 40 pounds at that point. I had started step work and was sharing in meetings, I was riding on a pink cloud and feeling good, wasn't even craving anymore! I knew I was supposed to stay for six months, but also knew my first pass was approaching and was thinking about trying to "convince" my parents I had learned what I needed to being there and would be ok to return home. I was excited to go on pass, it seemed like forever since I had been home and didn't have to wake up and follow a busy daily schedule. I knew they wanted a break from taking care of my kids and running my life for me, surely they would see I was serious now……."I've got this!".

After 90 days in treatment I was eligible for a weekend pass where my father could pick me up on a Thursday and have me back prior to visitation ending the following Sunday. If you were late you forfeited your next pass, so I knew I had better be on time. As I said I was anxious and excited to reach my 90-day mark and go home. With the work I had been doing on myself, I was processing a lot of guilt and felt this compulsion and need to fix everything and all of the wreckage I caused, as quickly as I could. I believed I was ready to take my life back and make everything better with the people I had hurt in just 90 days, and this pass would be my chance to show my parents how motivated I was.

One of the requirements of the facility I was at to gain approval for your first pass was that you had already completed your 4th and 5th steps in your step work. This was to provide additional incentive/motivation for all of us to maintain focus on completing our step work to earn the privileges we wanted. Women from various home groups in recovery would volunteer their time to come and complete our 5th steps with us. Due to unknown circumstances a couple of the women had not been able to make it out to The Bridges and we got a little backed up with women waiting to complete their 5th step. Therefore, as my first pass approached, myself and a few others were told we would not be penalized and our passes would still be approved as long as we had completed all of our 4th step paperwork and were signed up to complete our 5th step at the next available opportunity. I breathed an internal sigh of relief. Although I had been to treatment in the past and been in and around the rooms of recovery, I had managed to avoid ever completing a 4th and 5th step.

If you aren't familiar with the steps, the 4th step is to, "Make a searching and fearless moral inventory of ourselves" (AA Big Book, p.59). When completing this step, you make a thorough inventory of your resentments, sexual inventories and look at what emotions are driving your behaviors and why. You have to be honest about your defects, be willing to be completely honest, look at your part and your actions and remove the word, "blame" from your vocabulary. Then, it is followed with step 5, "Admitted to God, to ourselves, and to another human being the exact nature of our wrongs" (AA Big Book, p.59). This one terrified me! I can remember thinking, "You want me to tell all of my dirty laundry to another human being? In my experience most, human beings I knew could not be trusted and I thought telling them everything was just providing them ammunition to use against me or hurt me with in the future. Why can't I just admit to God and to myself, that should be enough, shouldn't it?". But I was wrong, and today am so thankful for finally completing these steps.

I was scheduled to leave the next day on my first pass. I was downright chipper completing my work in the kitchen that morning, even singing to myself. Then, a woman I love and admire deeply, the same woman that I have referenced throughout as loving me enough to tell me hard truths when I needed to hear them early in my journey walked in the kitchen, looked at me and said, "Let's go". "What?", I responded. "Go where?"......... she looked me in the eyes and said, "To do your 5th step, you go on pass tomorrow right? Gotta get it done". My mind started racing, I wasn't prepared, I thought I was ok to complete it after returning (and if things went the way I was hoping, I would not be returning), why me?..aren't there several girls that still need to complete theirs too? She saw my thoughts clearly in my expression and said, "Roxanne, just get your stuff and come on, you need to do this"........ and off I went.

I was physically shaking on the way over to the main house where we could have some privacy while talking and trying to quickly smoke a cigarette to calm my nerves. I remember feeling embarrassed; you could see my hands shaking while attempting to light my cigarette. She just looked at me and asked, "Roxanne…..I know you have been to treatment before…..how have you managed to never complete a 4th and 5th step?" and I honestly answered, "because I avoided it at all cost". She didn't say anything else, she just smiled at me…..and we walked into the house. I learned a lot about myself that day. I gained insight into my thoughts and actions, my behaviors and patterns to my resentments along with my motivations driving my unhealthy behaviors. I sat and thought……, "So that's why this is so important to do with someone else…..someone who gets it, without judgement and can be objective in helping you identify your part in things……what a blessing!!!" When it was over, I kind of thought I may throw up, but I also felt as if a 50 lb. weight had been lifted from my shoulders; it was an amazing experience. I had shared things that day that I had never said out loud to anyone before and slept better that night than I had in a very long time. I've learned to "name the dragon and take its power" as one of my favorite people always says. When you finally say things, they lose power in your thoughts.

I left early the next day to go home on pass…..on top of the world. Shortly after getting home my happiness slowly started to change to fear. I was afraid to leave the house, because I might run into someone. Like my ex-boyfriend, who I knew was still using and thought I might be tempted to use with him. I was afraid to go to meetings because I thought they were going to judge me for my previous relapse and having to return. I was afraid to take a nap or act sleepy, because I worried my parents were going to think I was using. I started thinking about everything I discussed while completing my 5th step the day before and had the realization that I didn't have this yet..... I was just now beginning. It was a blessing to spend time with my family, confirm what I thought that my ex was still using, but the biggest blessing I received that weekend was the insight that I still needed to be in treatment and still had a lot of work to do. I never even discussed not returning with my parents. I knew now being in treatment was an opportunity and now understood when the other girls would tell me, "Stop counting your days, and make your days count". And that was what I intended to do when I returned.

When I got back I put aside the remaining ego I had not realized I was still carrying around. I got honest, regardless of how hard or embarrassing it was. I started asking for suggestions rather than simply complying when I was told to do something….it was uncomfortable, but I started to grow and it felt good…..good enough to want to keep going. I started relying on God and gained so much strength and peace, I was honestly in awe. My thinking started to change and I now told myself, "This is a lifelong journey, where you don't have to, but you get to continuously grow and improve…….it's not a destination…..I will never 'have this'". Again, someone I love and respect often says, "Drinking and drugging are just symptoms of an underlying problem…..your drinking and using didn't get you to treatment......your thinking did." And my thinking was finally starting to change.

Somewhere around the four and a half months mark we had a guest speaker from my hometown come to visit. He immediately gave me an update on my ex. His motives were to reinforce to me that I had made the right decision and encourage me to continue to stay away from him if I wanted to stay sober, he knew how well I had been doing and was worried for me. However, in that moment I was struck with jealousy.......yes jealousy! I was jealous that he was out there using, with the people we used to "run" with and I was "stuck in treatment". It was my first thought and emotion. Then I had to walk out back and start to cry......because I felt guilty that my first thought and emotion was jealousy and wanting to use…..I know better than that…...am I crazy?!?!?! Look how far I have come. I knew I didn't want to go back to that life and was so ashamed of having those feelings. I later talked to someone about it, and learned it was natural at the point I was in my sobriety and to not beat myself up…..it wasn't about having those thoughts, it's more important to look at what I do with them that is different today, and that made sense to me.

About a week later I started struggling to sleep again and was having night terrors almost every night from my PTSD. I felt so defeated and frustrated. I thought I had made great progress…..why was all of this happening now?!?

But instead of staying in my head about it like I would have in the past and obsessing, I did something different this time and talked to someone about it. I prayed about it and turned it over to something bigger than myself. And contrary to what I had experienced in the past......it started getting better. I gained perspective talking to someone and was thankful God presented these challenges to me while I was still in treatment, surrounded by support and in an environment where running from my emotions and using was not readily available. Again, my thinking changed. Instead of remaining angry or feeling like a victim, I found gratitude.

The more and more I started to see the differences in myself and my relationships with my family and loved ones, I was motivated to keep going and pushing. The next month or so seemed to fly by! I started reaching out to and helping some of the newer women when they arrived and started to feel better and better……it was unbelievable. Deep down I started this process thinking I was special, or as some say, "Terminally unique"; that I was going to prove that this wouldn't work for me. But thank God, it did work and continues to everyday……as long as I remain willing to do my part.

My thinking continued to change and become clearer the longer I was there and the longer I maintained my sobriety. When I heard updates of my ex using, I now felt sorry for him and was overwhelmed with gratitude for that not being me anymore……I stopped having a reaction of jealousy the more I progressed in my life of recovery. When my parents questioned me or my motives, I no longer became defensive and argumentative, rather I became transparent and understood that I created their distrust and my actions and time would be needed to rebuild it, I looked at being a mother as a privilege rather than taking it for granted. My decision making, judgement and reasoning had changed dramatically in only six months, I was amazed.

But now it was time to go home…..was I ready? Could I maintain and be successful once I left my bubble? Would I trust a sponsor the way I trust my friends here in treatment? Will I be able to implement all of these tools they taught me once I am back home in my old environment? It scared me to think about it, but I knew it was time and I had the ability to be successful…..I had the choice now, I just had to make the right one. I had learned how to face my fears, navigate through them and come out stronger for it on the other side. Now it was just time as they say for "the rubber to meet the road".

The day before I left, I stood at a podium in front of about 50 women. It was a requirement to complete treatment to tell your story and share your experience, strength and hope with your peers. Although I had shared throughout my time there, I was intimidated to stand in front of everyone and tell it. I managed to get through my story only crying briefly once or twice and then it was done. The next morning, I stood in front of everyone at that same podium and read the 7th step prayer, hugged everyone and hopped in the truck with my Dad to head home and begin the next chapter of my journey. It was a bittersweet moment. The six months I thought would never end when I arrived had flown by in the blink of an eye looking back. I cried pulling away as my peers lovingly sang "Hit the road Jack…..and don't you come back no more, no more, no more, no more" (Ray Charles, 1961). It was a tradition of sorts. Of course, you were always welcome to visit, but the manager made a point to tell me never to return as a patient, I had come too far, and my boys needed me……and she was right.

Chapter 5

I Have a Disease????

It's not an excuse…..or a cop-out….

I remember being told I had the disease of addiction. I did not buy into the concept that addiction was a disease. I felt like that was a "cop-out" of sorts. Yes, I used and drank to the point I was physically dependent, but I wanted to drink and use, and sought it out for a very long time. There had come a point, as my addiction progressed where I did not want to use anymore but had to. However, I saw this as evidence that I was morally bankrupt and hopeless, not that I had a disease. I had sat comfortably in a victim role and mentality for a very long time throughout my active addiction. Again, my thoughts were, "If you had been through what I have been through, you'd get drunk/high too". When I was finally ready to give my best effort to get and STAY sober I thought that saying I had a disease was still "playing victim" and using an excuse for my behavior and actions and that I needed to be accountable. If I accepted what they were telling me……that I have a disease of addiction……I thought I wouldn't be able to still really be accountable, but I was wrong.

I opened my eyes and instantly thought…. I need drugs, I'm hurting…..but I'm broke….what can I sell? Do I have enough gas to get to the pawn shop? I wonder who has something today…..wait what day it is? UGH… I am so sick of living this way,

I'm over it, I'm done, ENOUGH. I don't care how sick I get, I know it only takes three to four days to get this shit out of my system…..I'm stronger than this…..I DON'T CARE HOW BAD THIS GETS!! They told me once in the ER that heroin withdrawal will make me feel like I'm dying but it won't actually kill me. I'm doing this, NO MATTER WHAT! I looked over at the clock…..it read 5:23AM…...DAMMIT, I wish I could just sleep through this and I start to stare at the ceiling and think about ANYTHING else other than using…..but can't. I've made it through things that should have killed me…..I can do this too. I DON'T WANT TO USE ANYMORE…..it doesn't work anymore anyways. I'd rather go through this or die then continue on this way….UGH…..I can't die….what would that do to my boys? I just have to suck it up and do this!

I'm freezing……then ten minutes later I'm soaked in sweat…..then the chills come back. My nose and eyes are running like a facet….my mind starts to wander that I can convince my parents that I am sick and need money to go to the doctor or get some medicine, they know I don't have health insurance….they'll probably feel bad for me and try to help me out….wait….NO! I am doing this….mind over matter…..I am NOT DYING, just lay here sweat and hurt Roxanne…..your babies deserve better. Mom and Dad would DIE if they actually knew what I was doing…..I HAVE TO STOP THIS. Then I run to the bathroom and start having diarrhea and throwing up into the tub at the same time. I hurt all over……EVERYTHING hurts. This is hopeless, I can't do it……DAMMIT!

I lay back down, feeling like someone is twisting my stomach into a knot….I groan in pain and attempt to focus on something and get thru this…..I repeatedly tell myself NO, DAMMIT ROXANNE…..NO, YOU CAN DO THIS. But I can't…..I look over and see it has only been 3 hours, and became overwhelmed with a feeling of defeat…..how will I ever make it 3 days…..I guess it is what it is….I'm just a junkie, it doesn't matter if I want it or not anymore…..I NEED it! It's now almost 8:30 AM…..I'm sure someone is up by now, let me just make a call and see what I can work out….maybe I can just try to wean myself down…..It's probably worse for me to stop cold turkey with as much as I was using anyways….."

    I remember at one point I was drinking about half a gallon of rum a day. I knew if I drank it all before morning I would be sick and shaking. I would tell myself I needed to pace myself and just drink enough to relieve my withdrawal symptoms. I didn't want to be sloppy drunk….I just wanted to get to the point I felt good and was free from the prison in my mind. I would take a marker and draw a line on the bottle to remind myself, in case I got too drunk later, to not drink past that line. I was determined to manage my situation and had a fail proof plan in my opinion. When I woke the next day the black line I drew was still on the glass of the bottle, however the bottle was always empty.

My addiction and compulsion to drink overrode my ability to reason. This is the concept I was talking about earlier, when my addiction progressed past the point of wanting to drink or use to HAVING to drink or use. For any of you reading this book that have experienced the same, it is a miserable place to be and not living. But there IS hope, you aren't hopeless……you're an addict/alcoholic that has the disease of addiction.

It was after I had started working in a treatment center and was given an opportunity to sit in on a group where a therapist explained addiction and the concept of the "Hijacked Brain" before I can say I honestly bought in completely to the disease model. I think it was very important in my recovery to fully understand what was happening before I could fully attempt to forgive myself and move forward. That doesn't mean my actions didn't hurt people and that I didn't have amends to make and things to take accountability for, but understanding did wonders for me.

I am FAR from a scientist, but in my experience once people started talking over my head when discussing the disease of addiction and the brain, I usually checked out and didn't take much away from it. So, I thought I'd share my understanding of the disease of addiction and how it helped me in my thinking and understanding in relation to my recovery. Addicts and alcoholics are not bad people who are evil or morally bankrupt. The therapist that presents the Hijacked Brain so well that I referenced, starts every time saying just that…..and to, "Hate the addiction…..not the addict!"

By definition a disease is something that causes a measurable change to a bodily organ, in addiction that organ is our brain. When you are diagnosed with a disease your symptoms are examined right? So let's look at the symptoms…..lying, manipulating, stealing, isolating, breaking laws, etc., etc. Even though the specifics of our stories vary some…..if you watch other alcoholics and addicts while listening to someone share their story you will see a lot of head nods and people relating because they hear themselves and can relate to the behaviors being discussed while in active addiction. Regardless of background, race, religion, education level…..this disease does not discriminate and the symptoms are always the same.

To keep this simple, let's start with the frontal lobe of the brain. This is where we complete reasoning and decision making. We reason through decisions we make checking them against our morals, values, laws, benefits, consequences, etc. I cannot even count the number of times during my active addiction and in early recovery when I heard my parents say, "We did not raise you to act like this. You know better than this. I don't even know who you are anymore…..the Roxanne I know and love would never act this way." All of the values they instilled in me and moral compass they provided while I was growing up was still there….I was still Roxanne.

However, during my active addiction my brain had become hijacked due to my disease and I quit communicating with that part of my brain and started operating out of my midbrain, sometimes referred to as the "caveman brain" since it operates to ensure survival.

The midbrain is where or survival needs are managed. You may have heard someone in the past discuss "fight or flight mode" which comes from the midbrain in an effort to protect yourself and ensure your survival. We have a hierarchy of needs that are monitored by our midbrain such as food, water, sleep, breathing, etc. Your midbrain will send signals to your body to let you know what you need to survive. When I need food, my stomach will start growling and I might feel a little weaker. When I need water, I start getting thirsty and my mouth may get dry. When I need to sleep my body will start to slow down and need to stop moving and rest. The midbrain is so powerful that even when I am sleeping it continues to keep me alive by telling my body to breathe. When you have the disease of addiction, at some point during your using and drinking your brain adds your drink or drug to the list of needs in your midbrain hierarchy, and the brain becomes hijacked so to speak.

As we are taught, the disease of addiction is a progressive illness, meaning it worsens over time and continued use. As our disease progresses the drink or drug moves up the list of hierarchy needs until it is number one, second only to breathing because that happens without any effort on our part. At the end of my active addiction I didn't care if I ate, I went with little to no sleep, I hardly even showered anymore......I had gotten to a point where if I was conscious my first thought was to use. To get more, and to continue to use......EVERYTHING else became secondary. My brain was now telling me I HAD to have my drink or drug to survive and would drive me to do things outside of my character to do whatever I needed to in order to obtain my drink or drug, and to lie, steal and manipulate in an effort to "protect" my addiction, because my brain was telling me I had to in order to survive.

Although this concept makes sense to most addicts and alcoholics because they have experienced it, even if they didn't realize what was happening, most family members and people who do not have the disease of addiction typically struggle to make sense of this. So, I enjoy using the example below to demonstrate how the midbrain takes over and will hijack your ability to reason while decision making that seems to help:

"Imagine you and I are very best friends. We have grown up together since we were babies. We went to daycare together, all through our school years we were always together and trust each other completely! I am a grad student and call you to ask for a favor. I explain to you that I am completing a study and experiment on how long someone can hold their breath. I start telling old stories of us when we were little going under water in the swimming pool and counting for each other and we are both laughing at the memory. I then proceed and explain that I need your help to volunteer for my experiment. I reassure you that I won't let anything happen to you and will keep you safe. I also explain that I was provided a grant to complete my study, so on top of everything else, you'll get $500 for helping me out. Given our history you agree to help immediately, you trust that I won't allow anything bad to happen to you and you get $500, why not!?!

Once you arrive for the experiment you see that you will be monitored by a machine and start to get a little nervous and intimidated, but your frontal lobe starts to reason through your fear and reinforces for you....this is Roxanne, I've known her my whole life, she would never let anything bad happen to me...and I get $500. Once you are seated I tell you that I am going to pinch off your nose and cover your mouth and see how long you can go without breathing before getting to the point of passing out, but again reassure you that I have equipment to monitor you and make sure you are ok and I wouldn't let anything happen to you. You start feeling uncomfortable and anxious but you again reason through that fear and anxiety in the frontal lobe of your brain....this is Roxanne, I've known her my whole life, she would never let anything bad happen to me....and I get $500....I'm ok.

So, then I pinch off your nose and cover your mouth and we begin. You are fine initially, and you start to think back of how long you were able to hold your breath at the pool in our younger years. After about 30-45 seconds in you start feeling more uncomfortable. Your chest starts to get tight and your brain starts telling you to breathe, but you continue to reason through that urge utilizing your frontal lobe….this is Roxanne, I've known her my whole life, she would never let anything bad happen to me…and I get $500….I'm ok. After about another 45 seconds to a minute later your midbrain is now pounding and screaming at you to breathe, it is demanding you breathe, because you need to in order to survive. Your brain starts racing, you start to sweat and feel panicked, however you continue to wait and try to reason through your compulsion to take a breath…..this is

Roxanne, I've know her my whole life, she would never let...then BOOM! Your hands shoot up and pull my hands off of you as you gasp and take a deep breath. Right then, in that moment your midbrain overruled your frontal lobe and ability to reason through the need and compulsion to breathe because your midbrain demanded you breathe in order to survive.

This is the same concept of what happens when your brain is hijacked in active addiction. We attempt to repeatedly reason through our actions since they conflict with our morals and values. I still know right from wrong. I know I shouldn't lie, steal, cheat, etc., however, at some point the midbrain overrides my ability to continue to reason through this and BOOM - I drink or use because my midbrain is telling me I have to in order to survive. Another way to explain this that is a bit cruder, but effective is something a friend of mine says to families of addicts in an effort to help them understand the compulsion to use or drink. He tells them to take an entire box of laxatives and tell them no matter what not to use the bathroom. If you love me you won't use the bathroom....no matter how much they try to not use the restroom at some point they will not be able to reason through and will HAVE to go and use the bathroom......that is how it becomes in active addiction.....even if I didn't want to anymore, I reached a point where I HAD to use and drink. I was essentially using against my will at that point of my addiction.

In hearing this you might feel overwhelmed or hopeless, but you shouldn't....again this is a hijacked brain in ACTIVE ADDICTION. The good news is that this changes; your brain can heal and once you are not active in your addiction anymore you have a choice......you will no longer HAVE to, then you are faced with working on and changing your thinking, so you are no longer consumed with WANTING to either. However, depending on the substance being used and the amount being used it takes on average, 6 months to 2 years for your brain to fully heal and fire on all cylinders again in a manner of speaking, which is deceiving. The disease of addiction is the only disease that will tell you that you DON'T have a disease. Like I shared after only 6 months, my thinking was significantly changed, physically I gained my weight back and felt good, my color was back…..but I still had a year or more before my brain would fully recover from the amount of heroin I was using.

More good news! Although I have a disease, which a friend described to me once as "dis-ease", or "being in a state of dis-ease", there is a treatment for it, and it has been proven over and over to work. Again, I have a choice today. Yes. I have a disease that DEMANDS to be treated EVERYDAY. However, I have a choice today to TREAT my disease of addiction by living a life of recovery. If I CHOOSE not to treat my addiction by living a life of recovery, it will eventually demand I drink or use…..treatment is not optional.

Think of it like this. If I started feeling badly and went to the doctor and found out I have the disease of diabetes. The doctor would explain that yes, I have the disease of diabetes and it cannot be cured, however it CAN be TREATED. To treat my disease all I have to do is learn to change some of my behaviors and how I think about food and I can live a long, healthy life. He may tell me to start to exercise, to change my diet and stop eating sugar and to take some medicine every day. If I do those things, I will be fine. However, I REALLY like chocolate and my back usually hurts when I exercise, so I only take the medicine provided and don't change my other behaviors. By making that choice, I am only partially treating my disease and will most likely not live as long and as healthy of a life had I implemented all of his suggestions…..right?

This parallels addiction. Yes. I have the disease of addiction and it cannot be cured and never goes away. However, there is a treatment that I can implement and have a long and healthy life regardless of my diagnosis. I will have to take suggestions and modify some of my behaviors and thinking, but I can then live with my disease and have a happy and fulfilling life of recovery……why wouldn't I choose to treat it? Because my disease tries to tell me that I don't have a disease.

Like I said in the beginning of this chapter, understanding my disease helped me in my recovery and the importance of maintaining my program and spirituality to remain successful in sobriety and recovery. I was reassured to know there was hope, that I was still a good person. It was just going to take time and some work before everything healed and was fully functional again. But in understanding this, I became more open to take suggestions and surround myself with others that could help me on my journey, because I understood the NEED for it now. I am still accountable for all of my actions throughout my active addiction and since....my disease IS NOT an excuse....it's just a reality for me......that today I am blessed to be able to CHOOSE TO TREAT. If there is one thing I can tell anyone reading this, it's that it is SO WORTH IT, and you can do it too!

Chapter 6

Relationships

The difference between intimacy and sex…..and SO much more!

This is repeatedly the hardest topic to discuss with women in early recovery and what took the longest for my thinking to change about. Let me start by saying this…..if you are currently in a relationship, I am not here to tell you not to be, you don't have to defend anything. I know better than anyone what that is like and in all honesty if anyone told me I shouldn't be dating someone, that is the first thing I would have wanted to do and would have just to spite them and prove to them that they were wrong. I simply want to share how my thinking was and has changed and some boundaries I had to learn and establish to get to where I am today in my sobriety, and my understanding of a healthy relationship. I'm not here to tell anyone what they should do, I'm telling you what I had to do and how I established independence and gave up control. I became willing and my thinking, expectations and standards started to change too.

For so long I didn't know how to love myself. I looked to men and relationships to do that for me, to validate me. And as my mother always told me, "Roxanne…..two 'sicks' don't make a 'well'". What I thought was "love" just wasn't, but I didn't know anything different, and honestly didn't feel worthy of anything better. I thought the love people talked about in movies and songs was just fiction……not reality….or any reality I would ever know. My thinking at the time didn't allow me to even be conscious of that. My denial was in full blown delusion and I believed that I was in love…..when I didn't even know the meaning of the word, I'm so grateful I do today. I had to learn in sobriety what I wanted in life, rather than what someone else wanted or wanted for me. I learned how to be ok alone, how to love and validate myself, how to be in a healthy relationship and most importantly how to have love and intimacy rather than just codependency and sex.

So many things are discussed in treatment and in early recovery and our brains are just beginning to clear. All I remember initially was being told I shouldn't be validating myself through men and I shouldn't be in a relationship for at least a year. I am a somewhat educated person, but honestly, I didn't really even understand what they meant by validation and the thought of being single for a year was a miserable thought because I didn't want to be alone with myself.....it was easier to let a man love me, tell me I was beautiful and cosign my thinking.....so I told myself I might try to go awhile, but I'm not putting a timetable on it....."That's ridiculous", I told myself, "They don't know me, I'm different". Again, my thinking rationalized so much I believed I could still pick and choose what rules or suggestions I was willing to follow and believed I knew best and would be successful…..My ego and unwillingness to change my thinking out of fear of being alone caused me to stay sick.

So, what does validation mean? Well the definition of validation is: "Recognition or affirmation that a person or their feelings or opinions are valid or worthwhile. - 'they have exaggerated needs for acceptance and validation'". Well how does that relate to me and my recovery? For me, I didn't feel like I was loved or lovable unless someone else loved me and validated that for me, I didn't feel smart or successful unless someone else thought I was, recognized it and validated it for me….so on and so forth.

From doing step work and becoming willing to look at my part and motives in my past relationships, I am able to objectively look at my past today and learn from it, however, when I first got sober…..I wasn't capable of that at all. I was in a marriage that functioned more like a friendship and roommates for years, after that abruptly ended with his death and infidelity, I immediately jumped into an even unhealthier relationship. I can see now that he was a distraction from dealing with pain and grief I didn't know how to handle. He drank and used and was focused on partying and "having fun". He was an escape…..and the complete opposite of my husband. Throughout the abuse I endured during that relationship my insecurities, lack of self-esteem and inability to be happy and independent increased exponentially.

Once I entered treatment the first time I wasn't convinced I was ready to stop drinking and using completely but wanted to and needed to. But again, I was in a meeting and met a man. When looking at my motives again, he was older, had more sobriety than me, was big and scary so I felt protected and safe. He told me I was pretty, that he loved me, distracted me and made me "feel good" physically when I no longer had drugs and alcohol to do that for me. I was convenient for him too but could not admit that to myself at the time. I had a home, a car and a job……he had a duffel bag. I remember getting a sponsor and her telling me that I couldn't/shouldn't be dating him…..so I fired her about 24 hours later. She later told me I was going to be dead within a year, and I told her she was bitter and mean and got a different sponsor that wouldn't challenge me as much and I could manipulate easier. Although I was angry with her, and still don't think she had the best approach, today I understand why she felt the way she did and it is only by the Grace of God that I wasn't dead a year later….because I was using and drinking heavily again by that point. I later made amends to that woman, because today I can see she was just trying to help and was scared for me.

    I remember trying to convince everyone in my life the men I was choosing to be with were "good men", and that they were "good for me", but everyone saw through it eventually…..even me.

But I didn't believe I deserved or would have anything better or different. I have been told multiple times and by multiple people throughout my sobriety that my, "Picker is broken". I needed to stay sober for a while before trying to be with anyone. As much as I didn't like that, I knew it was true deep down. I now can see I chose relationships and surrounded myself with people I felt like were a little "sicker" than I was, so I could feel ok about what I was doing, and would even tell myself I was helping them, like I could save anyone….when I couldn't even save myself. But that is how I rationalized to be able to live with what I had become in my active addiction.

I was sitting there telling someone about my "fiancé", I had only been in treatment a few days and was getting to know people. I knew our situation probably sounded bad, but they just didn't understand and know us….that's not what it's really like I remember thinking and would go on and on explaining away any negatives and attempting to convince others that we were good for each other…..but I now know I was trying to convince myself. I was afraid to lose what was familiar, even if it wasn't happy or healthy, because it was all I knew and honestly didn't think anyone else would want me or love me for who I really was….especially now that I was in treatment and had admitted I was an addict as well as an alcoholic….on top of being a rape and trauma survivor and a widow…….I couldn't hardly say it all out loud at that point, much less believe someone that was healthy would accept all of those things without judging me…..but I now know that is because I was still judging myself.

I would tell people, "We are engaged….the ring is just in the pawn shop…." and try laughing it off. The reality was, even though he was eleven years older than me, his mother bought that ring and we pawned it repeatedly for money for dope. It was our "dope ring" rather than a symbol of love, commitment and a promise of marriage. I found out after some time into our relationship he was still legally married to a woman from his past, so us being engaged wasn't real anyways. But at that time, I believed in it, and was fiercely loyal to him and our relationship. I was misguided and placing him and our relationship ahead of my boys, my family and my health....but couldn't see that at that time. It took time for my thinking to change.

As much as my family wanted to forbid me from continuing a relationship with him and our goal of both getting sober and continuing our relationship, they realized at my age they couldn't really control that any longer, however they were able to establish boundaries and not support me in making poor decisions, and they did. I was angry at first, but am grateful today they loved me and my children enough to do so when I was unable to have the perspective I needed early on. I needed to come to the realization on my own that our relationship was not going to work....but it took time and work before I arrived there. Had I not, I believe I would be dead or in prison today.

He would send me letters in treatment...encouraging me....reassuring me he was working on his recovery.....telling me how much he loved me and wanted to support me in my recovery. And although everything I was learning about myself led me to believe otherwise I WANTED to believe him and ignored flags or evidence to the contrary for a while. He would position his recovery as being dependent on our relationship.....which I had learned wouldn't work long term. All it would take is us having an argument later on, and that would be a reason to use. I agree that it doesn't matter what motivates you initially to get sober, but once you start working a program that begins to change.....and for him it didn't. I would talk to other women I was in treatment with about it, and just tell myself, "Well, at least he's sober….he'll get there". I felt like I owed him something for loving me, which was because my self-worth and self-esteem was extremely low at that point.

I remember participating in a group one time and was asked to make a list of all of the attributes my ideal partner would have. It was a long list! I had this image of a dream relationship and how I would want to be treated and imagined as long as the drugs and alcohol was removed, it would be perfect. Then I remember the woman running the group looking at my list, turning it around and pushing it back to me saying, "Before you can expect those things out of a partner, you first have to possess them yourself". "WHAT?!?!", I thought. "Wait a minute here, I'll do it if I get it!". But that wasn't how it would work. I had to be the person I expected and treat people like I wanted to be treated....FIRST......and was told that, "you attract what you put out Roxanne". That hit me. I thought about that statement a lot. I was attracting people similar to what I was becoming, and my standards became lower and lower as my addiction progressed.

As I have said before addicts are not bad people, he was just sick like I was. I actually struggled more with moving forward and trying to love him from a distance because nothing catastrophic had happened outside of our using. I've talked about how my "normal" changed throughout the years. In all of my previous, unhealthy relationships my normal was that something bad happened to end the relationship. I felt valid in leaving the relationships due to "being wronged" and was able to move on due to being angry and a victim in my mind. That's not how our relationship ended…..he wasn't physically or mentally abusive. He was sick and manipulative and codependent due to his addiction. I struggled because I felt that sense of survivor's guilt or that I was leaving him for being an addict, which I was too. I felt like I was acting better than him because I was sober now. By not wanting to be with him, it felt hypocritical and unfair. But that thinking was unfair to me, to my family and mostly to my children. But more than being unfair, it just wasn't true…..it was just where my thinking was early on because I didn't know what a new normal would look like, be like and desperately was trying to combine my existing normal and comfort zone with a new normal out of fear. And the honest answer is it just took time, listening to people around me and focusing on what I could control and being healthy myself before those thoughts began to change.

Now, the subject most people get uncomfortable and shy away from talking about, but needs to be discussed and is a major issue for many women in some form or fashion in recovery, SEX. Let's just be real for a minute. If you are in treatment, early recovery or reading this because you want to quit and are just curious......ask yourself this......"When is the last time you had sex sober?"

I mean completely sober….no mood-altering substances whatsoever. If you were anything like I was, it had been a long time. I was learning that I needed to change the way I thought about sex but didn't know how. More than not knowing how, I was terrified too. I gained 60 pounds in 6 months when I got sober (which I desperately needed to gain) and was very aware now….of everything! I would jokingly tell other women that I now noticed I had, "Jiggle in my wiggle", I was self-conscious rather than confident as I had been in the past. I would worry that I wouldn't perform as well as I had in the past because of my decreased confidence and blaring awareness of everything now. I was questioning my motives when wanting to have sex to make sure I was not using sex for validation or to manipulate….that it was purely for love……MY HEAD WAS SPINNING! There was a lot more that came up for me about approaching a sexual relationship that I needed to talk about with someone who understood and I felt comfortable with, than simply stay away from relationships until you love yourself….there were many other dynamics I needed to talk about that I had never even thought about while in active addiction. I have PTSD, I have been raped…..what if now that I am sober something is triggered while having sex because I am more aware of what's going on? What if I freak out? What if I stay the night and wake up soaking wet with sweat having a night terror in front of someone? How will they understand that….I'll be embarrassed……I would get overwhelmed and think, "This is just too much….I'm damaged and broken…..even sober I am never going to be able to have a happy and normal relationship". This alone should have told me I wasn't ready to be in a relationship right away, but it didn't. My gut reaction was give up. I would tell myself, "There's no use, this is too hard, why try". But in sobriety I have learned to RESPOND rather than REACT. I learned early on that changing my thinking was going to take time and work, and that my first thought probably wasn't something I should be listening to. Utilize the tools and people in my life to respond to those thoughts differently, until my thinking did change……..and it did.

How did I start to change my thinking? Well first I had to understand my current thinking, which basically boiled down to I equated love with sex (Love=Sex) and sex with intimacy (Sex=Intimacy). Therefore, I put pressure on sex and made it bigger and louder in my head then I should have. I worried that if all of those worries of mine came true, then I would fail in my attempt to be in a relationship….based solely on sex. When most people think of failure, they may feel bad, or see it as a learning opportunity and move on. But for me (and many other alcoholics and addicts I have spoken to) failure meant devastation. Like the chicken little concept, "The sky is falling". Failure and fear of failure was so big, that rather than seeing it as a learning opportunity, my thinking would tell me, "Just give up".

The change in my thinking is that love, sex and intimacy are all independent of one another and have different meaning in different relationships in my life. One is not dependent on the other necessarily. First, I needed to understand intimacy. By definition intimacy is, "close familiarity or friendship; closeness". Yes, sex is considered an "intimate act", however intimacy is closeness and familiarity in a relationship…..with or without sex. I started to identify relationships in my life where I had intimate relationships outside of people I had sexual relationships with (close friends, my grandmother, my children) to give myself perspective on what constitutes intimacy, outside of sex. Then, I was able to approach relationships with men wanting to establish that same closeness and love without it being clouded by just sex and me equating sex with love and intimacy. Once I have developed an intimate connection with someone, love grows and is strong in that relationship. Once I had that in a relationship with a man, sex was just an intimate connection and expression of love for one another. It was a wonderful component of our relationship we shared…..not the entire basis of the relationship. Once I had that closeness with someone, I was able to talk about my fears and awareness. I talked about being nervous, my nightmares, etc. and he loved me through it…..and it wasn't nearly as big, loud and scary as I had made it in my head....when I was in a healthy and loving relationship. It was something I didn't believe would happen, but knew I didn't want to go back to living the way I was, so became willing to try to change my thinking.....and it turned out better than I could have imagined. I was 36 years old before I learned and really understood and appreciated what a genuine loving and intimate relationship with a man is. The reality is sober sex isn't scary or anything I needed to rush......it's wonderful and better than anything I've experienced previously, but that would never have been a reality for me if I had not changed my thinking and learn to love and validate myself first......regardless of how long that took. In my experience it was longer than 12 months.....but that's ok, it's worth it. I needed time to heal and be whole independently before I could be a part of a couple in a healthy way.

Today, I am in a relationship…..but I was impatient of course. Once I had been sober for a while and felt like I was happy and doing the right things, I wanted everything to happen like yesterday….immediate gratification. In active addiction I used alcohol and drugs to change the way I felt instantly…..and in sobriety I had to learn to have patience and allow things to happen in God's time rather than imposing my will and trying to force things quickly, and they work out better than I could have ever arranged when I get out of my own way. I remembered when I was told in treatment that we, "Attract what we are putting out". I remember getting so frustrated with being patient at one point that I called the woman and friend that ran that group and asked her, "Given the lack of relationship I am in, or the men that have been 'hitting' on or approaching me……what in the hell am I putting out there? I must be doing something wrong?!?!" and we both laughed before she reassured me and helped me gain perspective on my need for patience and focusing on my relationship with God, my recovery and my life with my children……I remember her telling me, "Roxanne, before you do anything….ask yourself, 'Does this feed my soul?', if the answer is no…….don't do it".

I'm very happy today and grateful for the man I share my life with. I never thought I would be with what I playfully call an "earth person" meaning not someone in recovery, because I didn't think they would "get it" or have acceptance for my past, but I was wrong. He supports my recovery and understands that without my sobriety and my program of recovery I wouldn't be the woman he fell in love with, so he supports me in an effort to help "protect" what makes me....me, rather than being jealous of me spending time on myself and my recovery. He sees my scars as strength and admires who I am today, rather than judging me for who I was during active addiction. I thought briefly, "This is too good to be true.....he must be a unicorn or something". But I learned how to let someone love me, and accept where I am today, rather than waiting on the other shoe to drop. I learned that love isn't a fairy tale, but it is genuine and fulfilling. I am worthy of love, happy and healthy today ……. because I learned how to change my thinking and love myself FIRST! I also learned that my happiness and sobriety are not contingent upon my relationship. My relationship adds to my life and happiness, however, if for any reason it didn't work out in the future, I would be ok and trust that it wasn't part of God's plan for me. I would still love myself and have my life, family and sobriety…..that isn't dependent upon someone else today, it's just enhanced by him being a part of it. And if I can do it…..anyone can do it, there is HOPE ladies!

Clint and I. My "unicorn", my love, my support and my heart. Who I am blessed to share my life with today. I am able to share an intimate and loving relationship with him now, because I learned how to love, respect and validate MYSELF first

Chapter 7

Coming Home

…Now What?!?!?!

I remember when I came home from treatment, so confident and at peace…..I couldn't remember the last time I had six months of sobriety and felt so much like a new and better version of myself. The closer we approached my home town, the more uneasy I began to feel. It was a strange feeling…..because I felt ready, I missed my boys, my family and my life….but didn't know what the future held and had never been successful for an extended period of time maintaining my sobriety and life on life's terms once going home in the past. I was nervous. I was getting used to feelings again and identifying them and why I was feeling them, but there was no denying this feeling.....I was nervous. Even though I knew I shouldn't still have feelings of entitlement, there was a part of me that still felt like there should be a parade waiting for me in my hometown for being six months sober and completing treatment.....for doing what other people manage to do every day without having to go to treatment......but my thinking was still, "If they had ANY idea how hard it was for me to complete treatment they would think I deserved a parade too....they just don't get it". Once I arrived home there was an element of almost not knowing what to do with myself. Like if I sat still and didn't move I knew I'd stay sober. I had been in such a structured environment with black and white expectations for the last 6 months but when it was time for me to implement that myself, I kind of just sat still not knowing what to do first.

I had a temporary sponsor, which was a woman from my hometown that would come to visit our treatment center periodically to do groups or step work with women in treatment. I came home, and everyone was hugging me and happy and trying desperately to make me feel at home again. It was well intentioned but awkward to say the least. But, I called my temporary sponsor, and she "normalized" everything for me, reassured me that how I was feeling was normal and got me moving. She asked me to go to a meeting with her the next day at the detox facility I had frequented in the past, and I did. I was nervous initially; I remember being less than gracious in my attitude and how I talked to some of the staff there when I was detoxing in the past. Plus I remember how miserable I was when I was there and was afraid it would take me back to that place mentally and emotionally....but my temporary sponsor knew better. I was able to get a big hug from the staff and make amends for my behavior in the past and saw that they were genuinely happy for and proud of me; they understood. I was able to sit in that same room and provide hope to people and have gratitude for where I was, not feeling negative, but a needed reminder of how quickly I could be back in that chair if I didn't do the work I needed to daily to maintain my spiritual condition and life in recovery. It was just what I needed. Although this meeting wasn't a sanctioned 12 step meeting of any kind, I regularly attended, and it was one of my favorite meetings I looked forward to each week.

I started trying to implement all of the things they taught me in treatment and making my recovery....mine and something that would work for me realistically and in my everyday life. That doesn't mean I loved doing all of it. Actually, it was the complete opposite for a while. I was that girl that would call my sponsor, KNOWING it would help and still hope I got voicemail so I could get credit for calling but not actually have to talk about my stuff! INSANE thinking. But I never would have found what things worked for me if I hadn't been willing to keep taking suggestions and doing things that were uncomfortable to figure it out. One of the times, early on that has always stuck out to me was again, the first time I was alone, in my car and trusted to just go to a meeting. Even with ALL the work I had done and changes I had made, I thought about getting high. I romanticized it…..started to tell myself it would be different, it would be cheap….no one would know. But I called my sponsor, went to a meeting and didn't use. I responded instead of reacting in the same self-destructive way I had in the past and got stronger because of it.

    Once I started attending meetings, I chose a sponsor. I have had women ask me, "How do you choose a sponsor? Why do you need one?", or simply state, "I'm grown, I don't need or want someone telling me what to do!". I had similar thoughts and questions early on. They told me in treatment to find someone to sponsor me that was female and had something I wanted….but what does that really mean? Just that, don't over complicate it. I started going to women's meetings to meet more women and hear them share while trying to find a permanent sponsor. I remember hearing the woman that later became my sponsor in the back of the room talking to someone before the meeting started and she had this deep, genuine and contagious laugh. I remember thinking, "I want to laugh like that sober". So, I started talking to her, listening to what she shared in meetings and prayed about it, then asked her to sponsor me.

It is COMMON to be uncomfortable in asking someone to sponsor you. However, I feel it is important for you to do yourself. Several times I have seen people recommend sponsors for other people or ask for them, I recommend you complete this yourself for several reasons, primarily though you are starting step one and it is a great practice in humility. I have experienced being afraid to ask someone to sponsor me and talked to several other women that felt the same way. I playfully tell them usually, "It's crazy isn't it? We weren't afraid to put our lives in danger to get drugs……but we are afraid to ask someone to sponsor us". Provides much needed perspective sometimes, but I tell you all of that to tell you that it is NORMAL to feel this way…..do it anyway, sponsorship has been a vital part of my recovery. As for being grown and someone telling you what to do…..that IS NOT what sponsorship is. A sponsor will share their experience with you, act almost as a guide while working the steps, be a sounding board when you need one, etc., but they will NOT tell you what to do, they give you suggestions based on their experience. Typically, if you see something in them and their life in recovery you want, you are willing to hear them out and see the benefits to taking their suggestions. However, you don't HAVE to. No one is telling you what to do, you are not giving up control. You are still in charge of deciding what suggestions to utilize or following and which ones you choose not to, you are in charge of your own recovery. But being willing to hear someone out that has more insight and perspective and understands what you are going through is priceless! I'm forever grateful today that I put my ego aside and listened to people and allowed them to guide me through early recovery.

After getting grounded in my recovery back in my home environment I wanted to focus on getting a job and health insurance, but I was torn because I wanted to "make up" for lost time with my babies due to feeling guilty for having to be away from them for six months while I was in treatment. Growing up my father taught us....if you don't have a job, going out applying, interviewing and looking for a job was your full time job until you secured one. Now that I was sober I thought that is what I should be doing. But getting grounded in my recovery needed to come first. I could have and was tempted to go back to doing the same type of work I had in the past because I knew I could be hired on quickly, have good benefits and make good money quickly…..but I also knew that workplace, pace and environment was not good for my sobriety long term…...so I changed my thinking.

I found a job that allowed me to drop off and pick my kids up from school, where I made ok money, but it wasn't about how much money I made. I had structure, accountability, people depending on me again…..and humility. I was a server at Huddle House during the breakfast shift……..and loved it. I talked to people all day and was able to work diligently on my step work and being involved in recovery while still having time with my children. I knew this isn't what I wanted to do forever, but it was a start until God revealed my purpose. And He did.

I remember my sponsor pushing me whenever I felt stagnant, frustrated or stuck....and she repeatedly told me, "Roxanne, God does for us what we cannot do for ourselves......but God isn't going to do for you what you CAN do for yourself.....you have to do the footwork 'Faith without works is dead'" (AA Big Book, p.88 and KJV James 2:14-26). And she was right, I was sitting still and, in my routine, out of fear for a while after getting home. But as I continued to pray, and do the best I could to stay out of my will and the best I could with what I had in front of me, rather than attempting to run the show…..things started happening I never would have expected. I remember being in treatment and being given an exercise to imagine my life a year from then and to write down 5 things I wanted to gain out of maintaining my sobriety for a year. They told us to keep that list and look at it in a year, and they told us we would probably have sold ourselves short and far exceeded those expectations….because you can't imagine the life sobriety has in store for you. I was skeptical at best but completed my list. It was harder than I thought to even think of 5 things….I wasn't sure what to expect out of sobriety and didn't feel like I really deserved good things at that point. Today I am glad I did keep that list and look back at it, it gave me such an appreciation for all the gifts sobriety had given me in such a short period of time…..and as someone I love dearly in recovery says often, "It just keeps getting gooder and gooder".

I worked on changing my thinking about various aspects of my life….my home environment, personal relationships, parenting, having "fun", being active in my spirituality, etc. I had to look at what my current thinking was, how I planned on shifting my perspective and changing my thinking about them moving forward in my sobriety and put an action item to that new way of thinking to start actively making a change. An example that may give you an idea of how I approached this was my home/physical environment. When I went home from treatment I knew I would be returning to the home I used in for a long time, that I lived in with other men besides my late husband, and it held a lot of bad memories. However, it wasn't just about me. This was also the home my boys grew up in, that they lived with their father in. It was a symbol of "home" and stability for them…….their "normal" was associated with that house. I owed it to them to give them time and stability once I was sober before moving them to a new house, even if I had associated negative things with being there. So, I changed my thinking and started to focus on the positives it offered them. So how could I actively change that thinking. There were several projects and home improvements I wanted to complete on our home throughout the years and didn't have the money due to my active addiction. So, I planned to complete those improvements to update our home and complete them with my boys input and help so we could create our new normal and home together….and it worked! I eventually moved, but after getting two years sober and allowing my children the time they needed to trust me again and feel stable first….and I was happy in my home rather than haunted by bad memories…,just by changing my thinking. Having an action item gave me a way to actively be conscious of combating negative thoughts when they arose and a plan of attack to maintain a positive perspective. It worked! So I started applying that in all areas of my life.

I think it's important to say not only can you do it, but IT'S WORTH IT. I didn't believe that early on, but was out of options and thought I could at least give it a shot…..figured it couldn't get any worse. But because of time, a program and my relationship with God…..I am happy and sober and can tell you wholeheartedly IT IS DEFINITELY WORTH IT and it is better than anything you could imagine! Do I still have cravings and nightmares occasionally? Yes. Did they decrease dramatically over time? Yes. The difference is what I do with them today, but it is important that I remember my consequences and that I am always going to be an addict and alcoholic, so I don't attempt to convince myself that anything would be different if I tried using or drinking successfully again. I remember when my one year celebration was approaching….everything was good, my family was proud of me…..I had just started a great job…..and even with nothing "wrong" I sat alone in my room that night reflecting on the last year, and for a brief moment I had a craving to smoke crack……yep…..I couldn't believe it myself...but I did. I started telling myself that there wouldn't be a physical withdrawal like with heroin, I could do it just once and put it down, etc. Then I stopped and thought it through, and what I had gained in sobriety wasn't worth losing…..I was able to think and reason through that urge then where I hadn't been able to in the past. But that takes time and work, which is why it is so important to surround yourself with a support system, tools learned in recovery and other people working towards similar goals to avoid falling back into old ways of thinking while you are giving yourself the time you need to heal.

I've been told it's normal to have cravings around your anniversary, which made me feel better about it simply because it was normalized. I wasn't a failure, it wasn't a measure of my dedication to my recovery or love for my family, it wasn't a sign of weak faith…….it was a normal thought for an alcoholic and addict at that point in their recovery……it's just what you do differently with that thought today. By sharing it, addressing it and changing those thoughts, I get stronger. I no longer "sit" in those thoughts and allow them to grow into a plan or romanticize why I should do it…..I LIVE my recovery every day! Something I heard early on that I have applied and has helped me is just taking a day at a time. There are 4 to 5 things that I do every day, and if I do those things…..I know I have a pretty good chance at making it to bed sober each day, then I get up and start over again the next day. Those things? 1. I get up every morning and pray. Not for myself but for others and just to show appreciation and gratitude for an opportunity to live another day and for waking up sober. 2. I complete a reading or meditate to allow myself time to quiet my thinking and listen to God. 3. I talk to another alcoholic or addict (either in recovery or not), to relate but also to get out of self and try to help others…..puts my thinking into perspective and my "problems" of the day don't seem so big anymore…I may have some inconveniences but the reality is I don't really have any problems today, and I am grateful for that! 4. I try to go to a meeting as often as I can…..meetings are kind of like my medicine….I always feel centered and refreshed after attending one. and finally, 5. I pray again at night and THANK God for another day! I pray for my loved ones and any sick and suffering alcoholics or addicts both in and out of recovery. I do other things day to day, and usually talk to God throughout the day pretty often…...BUT if I at least do those 5 things everyday….I have a better shot at staying sober that day.

After I reached a year sober my sponsor encouraged me to take a service position within my home group, I started sponsoring and helping other women...because my sponsor told me it was time....and it would hold me accountable to my own program because I wouldn't suggest someone do something if I wasn't doing it myself. I was working in a treatment center at that point too and decided to become certified as a drug and alcohol counselor (CDACI) and then go back to school online and finally complete my degree. Only this time rather than a Business Marketing major (or keg stands as my mother once joked) I now had a passion and goal. I am completing my degree in Psychology with a concentration on Addiction. I am using my experience to help others in various ways, and it is better than any high or drunk I've ever experienced!

Chapter 8

Trust and Parenting

The monsters we create...

In the past I can remember being told over and over how much everyone who loved me just wanted me to stop drinking and using. Once I was able to stop, then I had to acclimate myself into the family again, and with the responsibilities and gifts sobriety gave me. I also now had expectations to meet and live up to. I can remember thinking more than once in a moment of frustration or self-pity along the way, "What happened to the days where you just wanted me to get sober?!?!?" But those were weak moments, and me wanting to "cop out" rather than be accountable and own my situation. The reality is, getting sober is just the start. I created distrust throughout my active addiction, I created fear and decreased expectations…..but I needed to be able to own that and be accountable for it before it would begin to heal and change. I created those "monsters" of distrust and fear within my loved ones and had to accept it would take effort on my part and time for it to heal; that was my reality. They DESERVED much more than me simply to stop using. People talk about patience and tolerance in getting sober in relation to their cravings, etc. However, patience and tolerance extend beyond me. I had to accept the fact that I didn't deserve to be trusted yet and my "amends" to my family couldn't be fixed overnight.

I had said, "I'm sorry" too many times in the past, I now had to show it in my behavior consistently. How do you rebuild trust to become considered trustworthy? By displaying trustworthy behavior and being trustworthy in my actions....it's that simple, it just takes time. I needed to remember I had used, drank, manipulated, lied and deceived the people I loved for a long time, as much as I wished I could correct that right away, it was going to take just as long if not longer to rebuild it.

Trust is so easily lost and so very difficult to rebuild. But it isn't impossible. As I shared in my story I made an attempt to become transparent with my loved ones once I came home from treatment, not because I had to, but because that was the least I could do if it put their minds at ease after all I had put them through during my active addiction. It was honestly a relief to me too. There wasn't anything to hide anymore, I had emptied all of the skeletons from my closet and was able to just live and be. In the past when they questioned any of my behavior I would become very defensive. Usually because they were right. Or if on the off chance I wasn't doing anything I shouldn't have, I would get frustrated and say and think selfish things like, "Well if I am going to be treated like a criminal and junkie anyways, what's the point, I might as well go use!". But that was not how my thinking became once I got honest, started working a program of recovery and working to rebuild the trust in my personal relationships. It was more about accepting they wouldn't be afraid and question my behavior if they didn't love me and care about me. And they wouldn't have to in the first place if I had not displayed untrustworthy behavior while I was drinking and using. It just takes time, but it does get better.

I had my own home and was able to pay my own bills, however because it made them feel better about things when I came home from treatment my parents continued to live with me and my kids for a few weeks until they were reassured I was settled in and active in my recovery during the transition. Although I purchased my truck from my father and it was in my name, I added the stipulation to the car title to where I would be unable to pawn it without his signature, I continued to provide them all of my account passwords and information so they could see what money I was spending and where if they felt the need to or were concerned. I had my driver's license; however, my Dad would drop me off and pick me up when I went to meetings for a while to ensure I was going where I said and not meeting up with my ex while at the meetings I attended. If I needed to visit the doctor for any reason I would invite one of them or my sponsor to go with me to have support and ensure I didn't get any medications I shouldn't be taking. I would invite them to open/speaker meetings occasionally, so they could meet some of my new friends in recovery and let them participate in my recovery if they wanted to and eliminate the mystery of the anonymity of the program. And was open to anything else they asked me to do in an effort to remain transparent in my actions and put their minds at ease. The biggest difference however was they didn't have to ask most of the time, I was aware of the need and therefore willing to suggest doing things to relieve any concerns that might arise and they were appreciative not only of me doing these things, but that I offered to and they were not put into an uncomfortable position of having to ask me to.

Something else that comes up early on usually is learning how to communicate with one another again and accept that just because I am getting better doesn't necessarily mean that everyone in my life is getting better too. They had to learn how to be around the "new me" so to speak. I had to remember that I trained them how to interact with me throughout my active addiction and that had become their "new normal" too, so they had to learn how to interact with me again in a healthy way, and that can take some time and willingness to communicate openly in order to accomplish. Also, understanding that not everyone is ready to forgive you initially or may still be holding onto resentments due to my behavior. At times out of anger or frustration things would be said or brought up about my past. Reminding me that I had things I needed to make up for…..throwing my past up or using it against me out of anger. They were not trying to be ugly or malicious, it is just a reality that things like that get said out of anger at times, especially early on.

When it did, rather than internalize it and beat myself up I would talk to my sponsor, share at a meeting or reinforce to myself that is who I was, not who I am. I know today I can't control what other people say, do, think or forgive. I know my truth and can only control my actions and how I respond to things today. Other people's opinions of me are just that, THEIRS and really, it's none of my business today, I can only be the best me I can be every day and help as many people as I can, the rest is out of my control, and I can accept that.

Along with rebuilding trust with my children I also faced some challenges in parenting that I have learned can be pretty common in early recovery…..and although the challenges change throughout the years….my using and drinking changed the dynamic I have with my children today. Although it was difficult initially, I was able to utilize my history to benefit our relationship rather than parenting out of guilt. When looking at things I feel guilty for, the things that were the hardest to face and attempt to forgive myself for, were the things I did to my children, and them having to live through my addiction with me. There were times where I feared that I wouldn't be successful at enforcing rules with them, because who was I to say anything, look what I had done....I felt like a hypocrite.

Something I have heard women say in treatment before is, "Well they are so young, they won't remember any of this anyways". To that I say.... YET, they don't remember everything YET.

They will, and I promise you that you would be surprised at how much they do know and understand. And for those that truly are too small to know anything, the instability in their little lives affects them even when they don't necessarily remember why. I don't say this to make anyone feel guilty, just to make sure you are aware. During active addiction we live in a state of denial and delusion, and the reality is, even if you are removed from them….even your absence and all of your actions negatively affect your children.

I said previously that I took being a mother and my children's love for me for granted rather than seeing it as a privilege. Something I have learned since getting clean and sober is that yes, a child's love is unconditional……but respect isn't.

Although my children have always, and will always love me….I need to earn their respect, and during active addiction I almost lost it completely. My boys were 7 and 10 years old when I entered treatment for the first time, so they were old enough to understand for the most part and knew that Momma was sick and needed help. I can remember my youngest son, a short time after I came home that time looking over at a liquor store on the corner from the backseat while I was at a red light and he asked me (with his little 7 year old brain wheels turning), "Momma if that stuff is so bad….why do they sell it to people?" I was stunned….and actually used something I learned from treatment to help explain it in terms that made sense to him. I said, "Well Logan, you know how some kids in your class can't eat peanut butter because they are allergic to it? And if they do they get real sick?". "Yes", he responded. "But you can eat peanut butter and be fine, right?". "Yes ma'am, but I can't take it in my lunch because some of the allergic kids might get some on accident". "Right", I said. So, I continued, "Well Logan that is what alcohol is like for Momma. I'm allergic to it and if I drink any I get sick, but other people are able to drink it without getting sick like Momma because they aren't allergic to it". I held my breath not knowing what to expect from him next, but simply got an, "Oh ok". And that was it. Although I was relieved in that moment, I also learned, as things came up it was important to do my best to be open and honest with them while also trying to explain things in a way that helped them understand.

Let's face it, they were very confused. At school, church and with all the other adults in their lives, all they have ever been taught is to not drink, use drugs or smoke....because it is bad, and bad for you. However, their little minds and hearts were conflicted because they loved and adored me and didn't think I was bad, I was their Momma. But they also knew I had to go to treatment because of drinking and drugging, and that was bad. So, bless their little hearts....me being open and honest when answering their questions was the least I could do for them. Even if I was embarrassed by my actions or felt guilty that they felt the need to ask questions in the first place.....it wasn't about me at that point. They had no choice when they were subjected to living with me during active addiction, so they deserved for me to include them and not shelter them from my life in recovery.

Something I also struggled with early on is how to not parent out of guilt and be the authority figure that I always should have been for them. While I was in active addiction there were many times that they did things without me knowing, for example my youngest son told my mother once, "Just ask Momma once she falls asleep on the couch and she will say yes to anything…". They also became more self-sufficient than they should have been at their ages due to my inability to be engaged fully while I was drinking and using. Not only did I feel guilty for this, I also encountered resistance from them when re-establishing my role as their parent. As much as they wanted me back, and to have a sense of stability and "normal" again, they also did not like it when I was alert and fully correcting their poor behavior again.

Early on my boys were not use to me holding them accountable for their behavior, and due to being in treatment for extended periods of time when my parents had to step in to be their primary caregivers, it was an awkward transition when I returned home and attempted to start parenting them again. They had experienced times when I was unable to care for myself, much less be able to care for them......so they didn't trust it initially, and it took a while for them to feel secure and stable and not constantly be waiting on the other shoe to drop. My mother told me once that my oldest son had confided in her privately that, "Granny, you know she's going to do it again…..it's just when". As much as it hurt to hear that…..that was my truth and I had to face that reality. His feelings toward my ability to maintain were valid based on what he had experienced and lived with me for several years, and until I was able to be honest with myself and face that I couldn't move forward.

It's tempting, out of guilt and lack of presence to assume more of a sibling or friendship role with your kids early on. I caution you NOT to do this….yes, this may seem easier and will make you feel better….but it isn't what they need or want. They need a parent…..not a best friend, and in sobriety I had to learn how to not allow my past to dictate how I parent today. Is it always easy? No. But it's my job. And today I have both the love AND respect of my children and a great relationship with them. I know better than anyone, what allowing them to feel like a victim and enabling and catering to that behavior can do. Yes, they have experienced things (the loss of their father, my addiction, etc.) that I wish they never would have and would change in an instant to protect them if I could….but I can't. The best thing I can do is use my experience to help them and raise them the best way I know how to moving forward. Life happens, no matter how much we try to protect our children, so I live as an example of working to overcome adversity today, rather than allowing myself to become a victim....which is the best lesson I can give them to prepare them for the rest of their teenage years and in the years to follow.

Although I am the parent, and they do not get to dictate adult decisions, it is important to be aware of and respectful of the situation we have created. Lack of trust, security, respect, etc. is normal, and no it is not ok, but understanding where it comes from and that I created that monster allowed me to find patience when needed and motivated me to ask for suggestions and guidance as I have faced challenges from other women that have been through the same things. Dating for instance. My boy's experiences of me dating after my husband passed away were negative. They witnessed drinking, physical violence, drug use, etc. and both times the relationships ended with me having to leave and go to rehab. They finally felt like they had me back and were terrified for me to ever date again….and saw all men as potential threats. Was that valid? Yes, however was it realistic at 34 years old that I would never want to be in a relationship again…..no. So I was sensitive to their fears….taking things slow and not subjecting them to someone until I knew it was something I was going to engage in long term, etc. They still did not like it initially, but once they saw and believed that my fiancé was not a threat and was genuinely a good person to me and them….they were ok…..it just took time.

There have been a few times when my oldest son got caught doing or saying something he shouldn't and when I addressed it, he would use my past against me or throw things I did in the past in my face. He wasn't doing this just to be mean or malicious, rather he was lashing out because he thought I would feel guilty and back down from holding him accountable for his behavior. It hurt when he did, but by me being consistent and not allowing him to use my past against me he learned that behavior is ineffective, and it stopped. In time he actually apologized for the things he has said and done in the past, because as I grow in my recovery….so does he…..and he is an amazing kid, I couldn't be more proud than I am of both of them.

Again, it isn't always easy...but it is completely worth it, and my relationship with my boys today is the best gift I have gained out of sobriety. Today I am a good mother. My boys have boundaries and clearly know right from wrong and my expectations. They have predictable and consistent consequences if they don't meet those behavioral expectations. They share in my life in recovery and celebrate milestones with me beaming with pride today. Since starting this book I celebrated my three-year sober birthday and my oldest son proudly stood at the podium and presented me with my medallion and said, "Mom, I love you and I'm proud of you". I know the future will undoubtedly hold additional parenting challenges, but with faith and my support network

I know I can handle things as they come....and not have to allow guilt to change how I parent.

My parents and I sharing time in sobriety. Living amends and rebuilding trust and a relationship is a lifelong process! They are PROUD of me and who I am today! Without their love, support and ability to set boundaries with me, I wouldn't be here today! Love you Momma and Daddy

Chapter 9

Giving Back

To give back to others what was so FREELY given to me….

How selfish would I be……if I did not want to share my experience because it is embarrassing or out of fear of judgement? I have found, just as it states in recovery literature that there is no power greater than one alcoholic or addict helping another. That was true for me, and if I had not found hope in someone that I was able to trust and relate to, I believe I would be dead today……I am so very grateful that God brought that women, and many others since then into my life to learn from and find hope in. So, I had a passion to do the same for other women as well. I honestly didn't plan on working in recovery, or working towards being a therapist......I just knew that God put it on my heart to share my experiences and use them to inspire others in sharing my testimony....and it grew from there.

    I learned while I was in treatment that the best way for me to get out of my head and stop feeling sorry for myself and my reality was to get out of myself and listen to someone that needed to talk. It ALWAYS helped when all else had failed. I learned that my problems were not quite so big and loud, and I was always able to find some perspective when I tried to be a friend to or listen to someone else talk about their concerns. There is a connection that unless you have experienced I can't really explain. Most women in treatment or early recovery are conditioned, usually out of survival, to not trust anyone fully, to be guarded. And being able to look at someone and genuinely tell them you understand how they feel, that it is ok and there is hope……that moment and ability to share in that with someone is better than any high I have ever experienced…..it's priceless and it helps me just as much as it helps them. I am able to remember how quickly I could be right back to where they are if I do not continue to make my recovery a priority…….and have gratitude for where I am today rather than taking things for granted at times.

When returning home from treatment, I joined a homegroup, found a local sponsor and started over in my step work. I remember an activity she gave me to reinforce my behaviors and practice looking at my motives when completing step one. I was actively practicing humility by doing something for someone every day, however without them knowing I had done it for them. No recognition for doing something nice or helpful for them. Therefore, I was being selfless and my motive for helping others was not about me getting recognition, etc. I LOVED this assignment! I found such joy in helping others, purely to help them….no other reason….so I knew then, my passion was to help people….I just didn't know how or in what capacity yet, so I explored it.

When I first came home I started looking into programs at local hospitals to be a victim advocate for women that presented in the ER after domestic violence, etc. It was a way I felt I could use my experience to help other women during a painful time. I wanted to help others with addiction as well, I honestly just thought it would take too long to go back to school to be able to work in a treatment center. However, while attending a meeting I met someone who recently started working at a newer treatment center in my home town and was telling me all about it. Before I knew it I was working there, completed my CADC (Certified Alcohol and Drug Counselor) and enrolled in college courses online to finish my degree and work towards becoming a therapist and now am also a Certified Peer Support Specialist in Mississippi. Much different than anything I had imagined for myself in the past. But it has inspired me and lit a passion unlike any other type of work I have ever been in.

Really all I did was I got out of the way, accepted God into my life and allowed Him to work through me. There is a prayer I say every morning since I was in treatment....in the AA program it is referred to as the third step prayer, "God, I offer myself to Thee - to build with me and to do with me as Thou wilt. Relieve me of the bondage of self, that I may better do Thy will. Take away my difficulties, that victory over them may bear witness to those I help of Thy power, Thy love and Thy way of life. May I do Thy will always." When I got to treatment this prayer was said aloud by everyone in treatment there every morning, and at some point, I stopped just saying it, and started praying it. It became a way of life for me that I am so grateful for today. All I can do, is my absolute best at what is placed in my path and leave the rest up to God.

There is a group I loved to sit in on that a therapist I love, and respect taught about our legacy...the legacy we are leaving and our ability to change our legacy. If I am able to help just one person get their lives back....their families and loved ones lives are touched and changed, anyone they help moving forward and their families and loved ones lives are changed...so on and so forth. THAT is a legacy I can be proud of today! I don't have to live feeling guilty of my past or wallowing in past hurts. I can focus on making a positive impact, helping others, being a good mother, wife, step-mother, daughter, sister, aunt, Christian, etc. and leave a legacy that everyone that loves me can be proud of....and that is AMAZING!

I was always a math and numbers person and only made it through my PSYCH 101 class in college when I was younger by volunteering as a "guinea pig" of sorts for the grad students and getting extra credit. I never imagined I would be studying towards a Psychology degree or writing a book! But, I am writing this book as a way to provide hope to women that may feel the way I have at some point in the past....and let them know how good life can be in sobriety....THERE IS HOPE

AND IT IS WORTH IT! In the last couple of months, I've teamed up with some others I know and love and started a charity to help women in need of treatment without health insurance or the financial support to get treatment for their addictions called The Penny Project. I've included information about the project at the end of this chapter and the proceeds from any sales of this book are being donated to that cause -- to get housing, life skills workshops, support and stability and good addiction education and treatment to women that need it and probably could not get it any other way. Today I am so grateful for my life, that I have dedicated my life to helping others find their ways out of the grips of addiction. There is value in learning about ourselves, building a relationship with God, seeking treatment for dual diagnosis, being financially stable….and although ALL of those things are needed, when learning how to not only GET but STAY sober…nothing is more helpful than someone who can show you the way that has been there before. It reminds me of a story that I love and impacted me the first time I heard it below:

"AN ADDICT FELL IN A HOLE and couldn't get out.

> A businessman went by and the addict called out for help. The businessman threw him some money and told him to buy himself a ladder. But the addict could not buy a ladder in this hole he was in.
>
> A doctor walked by. The addict said, "Help! I can't get out!" The doctor gave him some

drugs and said, "Take this. It will relieve the pain." The addict said thanks, but when the pills ran out, he was still in the hole.

A well-known psychiatrist rode by and heard the addict's cries for help. He stopped and asked, "How did you get there? Were you born there? Tell me about yourself, it will alleviate your sense of loneliness." So, the addict talked with him for an hour, then the psychiatrist had to leave, but he said he'd be back next week. The addict thanked him, but he was still in the hole

A priest came by. The addict called for help. The priest gave him a Bible and said, "I'll say a prayer for you." He got down on his knees and prayed for the addict, then he left. The addict was very grateful, he read the Bible, but he was still stuck in the hole.

A recovering addict happened to be passing by. The addict cried out, "Hey, help me. I'm stuck in this hole!" Right away the recovering addict jumped down in the hole with him. The addict said, "What are you doing? Now we're both stuck here!!" But the recovering addict said, "Calm down. It's okay. I've been here before. I know how to get out."

Author - Unknown

That is the POWER of giving back and the ability one alcoholic or addict has to help another. All of the other things that were given to the addict were needed and he was grateful for, however until he was able to get out of the hole....he couldn't utilize them to help himself. Anytime, anyone I have helped thanks me for anything, I simply say, "Thank YOU", and ask them to just continue to share what they have learned with others who need it too.....to pay it forward! That is the same thing I would like to challenge you as the reader to do also. Once you get this gift of a life in recovery....pass it along to another in need.....create your new legacy!

THE PENNY PROJECT

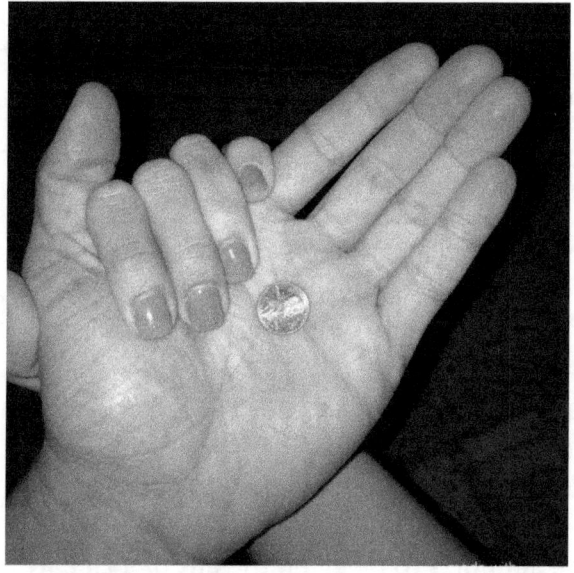

What is The Penny Project?

The Penny Project is a charity that has been organized to raise money and support for women recovering from addiction. It is focused on getting access to addiction treatment to women that do not have health insurance or financial support to get treatment. Not a traditional 30-day treatment but long-term support, sober living and life skills while maintaining their sobriety. Our goals include opening and supporting facilities in providing addiction education, family workshops, 12 step immersion, childcare if needed, life skills workshops (resume writing, interview skills, budgeting, parenting, etc.). We want women that wouldn't have the opportunity to gain access to these supports to be given the gift of a LIFE IN RECOVERY!

Who created it?

The Penny Project was created by The REINS Model Equine Therapy team. The REINS model was co-created by Dale Phillips and Clint Crawford. There are also other helpers within the team that support the therapeutic model and The Penny Project, to include myself and several others. Everyone involved is passionate about helping others and display genuine compassion. Not only is addiction treatment a focus of their treatment model, but also trauma and addressing what drives the addiction. When working in treatment centers it is common to have challenges finding placement for long term treatment for women period due to there being fewer options, and when they have no finances as well the task becomes nearly impossible. If we send people right back to the environments they were using in with little to no new skills that they have had a chance to implement with support, we are setting them up for failure -- we want to help people learn to maintain their sobriety!

How can I help?

There are several ways to help!

1. There is a book authored by Clint Crawford titled "A Penny's Worth of Compassion" that all proceeds are also being donated to The Penny Project fund - I've included the Amazon link below:

https://www.amazon.com/Pennys-Worth-Compassion-Clint-Crawford/dp/0692964428/ref=sr_1_1?ie=UTF8&qid=1512997695&sr=8-1&keywords=clint+crawford

2. You can make donations (Go Fund Me or PayPal), buy books, share our posts on Facebook (The Penny Project), buy and wear the Penny

Project bracelets and help spread the word and gain support.

3. Provide a review -- by writing a review on this book, or any of the REINS Model materials you are helping us to promote our cause and help spread the word!

4. Place a donation jar at your business or ask for local business owners to participate! By placing a Penny Project flyer and a jar in all of our local communities we can spread awareness and raise money to support this cause -- EVERY PENNY HELPS!!!

There and endless ways to help and show support, please reach out if you are interested in helping. We would LOVE to hear from you. This is an "US" project -- By doing something good for someone in need and you can make this a part of your LEGACY too!!!

Meet the REINS Model Team

What is The REINS Model?

Who created The REINS Model?

Dale Phillips and Clint Crawford (short bios below)

Clint Crawford has a long history of working in addictions and mental health dating back to 1997. Clint has worked with a variety of populations as well including children, young adults, adults, and geriatric patients. He holds a bachelor's degree in psychology, a master's degree in healthcare management, and a master's degree in professional counseling. He is the co-founder of the REINS model of equine therapy which specifically targets addiction and trauma. Along with his partner Dale Phillips, Clint has been asked to be a keynote speaker twice for the Mississippi Association for Addiction Professionals where they received perfect ratings both times. He along with his partner were also keynote speakers for the 2016 Masters Addiction Conference as well in Augusta, GA which was simulcast nationwide as well as in three foreign countries.

Dale Phillips is the co-founder, along with his partner Clint Crawford, of the REINS model of Equine therapy, a module specifically designed to target, and treat addiction and trauma. Dale is certified in equine psychotherapy and has both worked and spoken across the country in multiple venues about the power of equine therapy and the healing that comes from it. Dale has been featured in People's magazine specifically for his trauma work and is known both for his powerful individual work with patients, as well as his incredible group work for both patients and professionals alike. Along with his partner Clint Crawford, Dale has been asked to be a keynote speaker twice for the Mississippi Association for Addiction Professionals where they received perfect ratings both times. He along with his partner were also keynote speakers for the 2016 Masters Addiction Conference as well in Augusta, GA which was simulcast nationwide as well as in three foreign countries.

What other books have Darkhorse publishing and The Reins Model team put out about addiction?

- A Penny's Worth of Compassion by Clint Crawford
- The Prison with No Bars by Clint Crawford
- Beautiful Scars of Hope by Roxanne Holt
- Beautiful Scars of Hope Workbook by Roxanne Holt and Clint Crawford

Clint Crawford and Dale Phillips..... two of the most genuine, authentic and compassionate men I have ever had the pleasure of knowing

References

An Addict fell in a hole - Parable - Author Unknown

KJV Bible - James 2:14-26; AA Big Book, p.88

Hit the Road Jack! - Ray Charles, 1961

4th and 5th steps -- AA Big Book, p.59

Easier, softer way - AA Big Book, p.58

I am Heroin Letter - Author Unknown

www.ingramcontent.com/pod-product-compliance
Lightning Source LLC
LaVergne TN
LVHW051111080426
835510LV00018B/1994